BRINGING SEX INTO FOCUS

THE QUEST FOR SEXUAL INTEGRITY

CAROLINE J. SIMON

IVP Academic

An imprint of InterVarsity Press
Downers Grove, Illinois

InterVarsity Press
P.O. Box 1400, Downers Grove, IL 60515-1426
World Wide Web: www.ivpress.com
E-mail: email@ivpress.com

InterVarsity Press® is the book-publishing division of InterVarsity Christian Fellowship/USA®, a movement of students and faculty active on campus at hundreds of universities, colleges and schools of nursing in the United States of America, and a member movement of the International Fellowship of Evangelical Students. For information about local and regional activities, write Public Relations Dept., InterVarsity Christian Fellowship/USA, 6400 Schroeder Rd., P.O. Box 7895, Madison, WI 53707-7895, or visit the IVCF website at <www.intervarsity.org>.

Scripture quotations, unless otherwise noted, are from the New Revised Standard Version of the Bible, copyright 1989 by the Division of Christian Education of the National Council of the Churches of Christ in the USA. Used by permission. All rights reserved.

While all stories in this book are true, some names and identifying information in this book have been changed to protect the privacy of the individuals involved.

The lines from "L'Hotel Terminus Notebooks," from OPEN HOUSE by Beth Ann Fennelly. Copyright ©2002 by Beth Ann Fennelly. Used by permission of W. W. Norton & Company, Inc.

The lines from "Reflections on Ice-Breaking" are copyright ©1931 by Ogden Nash, renewed. Reprinted by permission of Curtis Brown, Ltd.

Design: Cindy Kiple

Images: © Ilona Wellmann/Trevillion Images

ISBN 978-0-8308-3637-6

Printed in the United States of America ∞

 green press INITIATIVE InterVarsity Press is committed to protecting the environment and to the responsible use of natural resources. As a member of Green Press Initiative we use recycled paper whenever possible. To learn more about the Green Press Initiative, visit <www.greenpressinitiative.org>.

Library of Congress Cataloging-in-Publication Data

Simon, Caroline Joyce.
  Bringing sex into focus: the quest for sexual integrity / Caroline
J. Simon.
      p. cm.
  Includes bibliographical references.
  ISBN 978-0-8308-3637-6 (pbk.: alk. paper)
  1. Sex—Religious aspects—Christianity. 2. Christian
ethics—Reformed authors. 3. Sexual ethics. I. Title.
  BT708.S535 2011
  241'.66—dc23

                                                              2011032889

P   18   17   16   15   14   13   12   11   10   9   8   7   6   5   4   3   2   1
Y   27   26   25   24   23   22   21   20   19   18   17   16   15   14   13   12

For my sons and daughters-in-law:

Paul and Julie L. Simon
Matt and Julie Ann Simon

May your marriages be as blessed
as Dad's and mine.

CONTENTS

Acknowledgments

W̲ork on projects connected to this book began with a Jacob Nyenhuis Faculty-Student Collaborative Research Grant in 2006. Laura (Johnson) Morris, my student collaborator on that grant, was very helpful in identifying sources and as a stimulating conversation partner. Her comments were philosophically astute, and her questions always made me think harder. I am grateful for the support that Hope College provided, both through the Nyenhuis collaborative grant and the John and Jeanne Jacobson Endowed Professorship.

Students in several sections of my Sexual Ethics course at Hope College engaged in dialogue about material that eventually found its way into this book. Their frank observations and fresh perspectives informed my thinking in many ways. The first formal presentation of material for this project was at the University of Otago, Dunedin, New Zealand, in October 2008. I owe thanks to the Department of Theology and Religious Studies for their gracious hospitality and philosophical exchange, especially to Dr. Paul Trebilco, department chair, and Dr. Lynne Baab. The presentation I made at Otago was later expanded and published as "Redemptive Engagement with Cultural Conceptions of Sexuality" in

the spring 2009 issue of *International Academy of Marital Spirituality Review*. Some portions of chapter four are modified versions
of material first published in "Seduction: Does How You Get to
'Yes' Still Matter?" in *Philosophy, Feminism and Faith*, edited by
Marya Bower and Ruth Groenhout (Indiana University Press,
2003). I am also grateful for comments from David Zimmerman
and an anonymous referee at InterVarsity Press that improved the
final manuscript of this book.

   I owe several people special thanks. Lezlie Gruenler was a fan-
tastic editorial assistant in preparing more than one version of
the manuscript. I am very grateful for her careful attention to
detail and her intelligence. Conversations I had with Heather
Sellers about the craft of writing made me a better writer—though
I'm nowhere near Heather's league. Heather's advice, "Kill your
darlin's," helped me cut out many passages from drafts of this
book that I enjoyed writing. Those passages may find a home
somewhere in the future, but this book as a whole is better off
without them. My husband, Steve, was supportive and encourag-
ing, as always. Steve put up with my whining on days the writing
was going poorly (or not at all); on other days he put up with my
holing up in my writing room for hours. More importantly, Steve's
gift to me of four decades of marriage informs the material in
chapter two and the conclusion. Finally, I owe a special debt of
gratitude to my good friend Dr. Lynne Baab, Jack Somerville Lec-
turer in Pastoral Theology at University of Otago, for her faithful
encouragement during my work on this book. Lynne often be-
lieved more strongly than I did in the value of what I had to say
on these subjects; without her steadfast faith in this book it would
not have been completed.

Introduction

Men don't make passes at girls who wear glasses." I don't remember whether I had actually heard that little ditty by the time I was ten years old and heading for my first optometrist visit. I'm sure I had not heard of its original author: Dorothy Parker. But I clearly remember the glob of dread in my stomach, a symptom that I'd already somehow absorbed this message. If I flunked this vision test, I'd be wearing the shame of that failure on my face for all to see. Before I knew what a pass was, I knew it was a shame to not be worthy of one. Before I knew much about sex, I was molded by my culture's norm: for girls, how you are seen is far more important than seeing.

I failed the optometrist's eye test. I hated every one of my school pictures from then until I got contact lenses at seventeen.

I'm now old enough to say resolutely that it is childish to value my appearance more than seeing clearly. Besides, I've never relished fielding passes, even before my marriage (now in its fourth decade). Yet I switched back to glasses from contacts only after frames became both fashion statements and effective camouflage for the wrinkles around my eyes. The messages I had absorbed as a ten-year-old in the 1960s are not easily shed. "Put away childish things" is easier said than done. Aging happens willy-nilly; maturity is an ever-receding goal. And we are left puzzling over mysteries—large and small, important and trivial. Here's a small one (or is it large?): Why do we care about being sexually attractive to a broad swath of humanity even if we are not looking for new partners?

This is a book about sexual insight: the clarity that we can gain when we succeed in applying moral acuity to sexuality. It is also a book that acknowledges how difficult an achievement of sexual insight is. Sex is complicated and riddled with mysteries. And sexuality isn't just intellectually complicated; our sexuality is rife with moral complexities. Sex at its best is about integration and connection, but we know that many times people's sexual behavior causes problems for them and pain for others. Much of this damage is neither malicious nor intentional. People often simply don't foresee consequences or understand the effect they are having on others. Lack of sexual integrity will fog our moral vision about sex. Some part of us resists seeing clearly enough to know the full depths of our fragmentation. Sexual insight and sexual integrity rise and fall together. As a Christian I think that we all fall short of perfect integrity in all areas—sexuality is no exception. Because we all lack sexual integrity to some extent, none of us has perfect sexual insight. We are all more or less muddled about sex, at least some of the time.

In light of that, this project seems presumptuous. How can attempts at sharing sexual "insight" be more than cases of the blind trying to lead the blind? And even if one granted that some people have more sexual insight than others, is sexual insight the sort of asset that can be transferred from one person to another? Sexual insight might be like perfect pitch in music—something you either have or forever lack.

But sexual insight is not like perfect pitch. No one is born with it. And sexual insight, like physical sight, comes in varying degrees of clarity or distortion. Sexual insight is not an all-or-nothing matter. As in the case of physical sight, there are various strategies that can be undertaken to diagnose and cure distortions in our perspectives on sexuality. Optometry (which I use as a structural metaphor) is the art of diagnosing visual distortions and prescribing corrective lenses. Twenty-twenty vision is not needed in order to be an optometrist. In fact, my optometrist and I both wear glasses. But my optometrist knows far more about correcting vision than I do.

Acuity in the moral sense is difficult to attain in sexual areas, in part because sexuality is both pervasive and ambiguous. When is a touch sexual, as opposed to affectionate or ritual? The football player pats his teammate on the rear. The acquaintance briefly kisses your cheek. The person you had thought of as "just a friend" stares into your eyes and reaches over to nudge a strand of hair behind your ear. The caregiver helps the preschooler change clothes after an "accident." Which of these is sexual? We cannot remove all the mystery from sexuality, but some ambiguities can be clarified. This is important because sexuality should enable human connection and flourishing, yet all too often we bruise and batter one another. Seeing sexuality *better* can help us connect while avoiding mayhem. Moral vision applied to sexuality is crucial for sexual insight.

This book is for anyone who values sexual insight and isn't sure they've got 20/20 vision in this area. It is not just for young adults or adolescents. Yet some of what I'll be sharing with you I've learned through spending several years teaching a course called Sexual Ethics to college students. Students come to the course with a variety of attitudes. Some take the class because they like the idea of getting college credit for thinking about sex. Thinking about sex comes naturally to them, so this class should be a breeze, right? Some are interested in ethical reflection and are intrigued to find out what others in the class think about applying ethical concepts to sexuality. Some are already sure they know what ethics should say about sexuality and just want to make sure that the professor and their fellow students know the truth. Some, frankly, are taking the class just because it fits their time schedule and doesn't sound as daunting as Introduction to Physics. Each term the mix of students is different, but all of these students think they have increased their insight about sexuality by the end of the course. That's not because their instructor is brilliant. Their sexual insights arise out of the "ahas" and "no ways" and "get reals" and "so whats" of grappling with the different perspectives on sexuality. They become more self-reflective and become more aware of how complicated living with sexual integrity is. Do they still have much to learn? Of course. We all do. Sexual wisdom is an ideal, a mark toward which one strives—neither they nor you nor I have fully attained it, but we can press on together in search of it.

This book is a philosophical essay written by a Christian. Philosophy is an art whose name comes from two Greek words that together mean "love of wisdom." As a philosopher, I seek wisdom. Some philosophers think they've found enough wisdom in an area to write a treatise—a relatively comprehensive systematic account. Others, claiming to know less, write essays instead of treatises. The root meaning of *essay* is "an attempt." I will be making my best attempt at truthfulness, but I cannot hand you wisdom as a prefabricated package. For one thing, I do not have wisdom as a done deal or complete package, either for myself or for others. And just as importantly, part of wisdom is self-reflection, as the classical Greek's exhortation "Know thyself" reminds us. To know yourself you need to understand what matters most to *you* and why. Part of sexual wisdom is coming to know how much sex matters to you, what the sources of its value are in your life, and how sexuality fits into the array of all those things you care most about. Although seeking such self-understanding need not be a solitary exploration, some part of it must be a do-it-yourself exercise.

I, along with many—not all—of the students who have taken my Sexual Ethics course over the years, have been shaped by what I will be calling a covenantal view of sexuality. This view is integral to the Christian faith in its traditional forms, as well as to some other religious traditions. This view sees full sexual expression as an embodiment of the lifelong uniting of two individuals within one new, shared identity. For this reason, sexual intercourse should be reserved for marriage, and both premarital and extramarital sex fall short of God's intentions for human sexuality. Sex is serious business, both ethically and religiously.

The covenantal vision for sexuality is an audacious ideal. It seems especially audacious in a society where the average age of first marriage is increasing, where the average age for first sexual intercourse is decreasing, and where divorce rates are high, for Christians no less than others. To some the covenantal vision has appeared dangerously unrealistic. Within the church, there is certainly debate about the implications of the covenantal view for issues such as divorce, homosexuality and long-term committed relationships before or in place of marriage. From outside the church, looking in, the covenantal view of sexuality can look grim and judgmental. Poet Beth Ann Fennelly includes the following striking lines in one of her recent poems:

On organized religion:
The man walking his dog in the apartment's courtyard
Yelling "Shame!" every time it defecates.[1]

Are Christians who uphold the covenantal view judgmental? Judgmentalism is a disposition to derive satisfaction from making negative moral assessments.[2] This disposition is rooted in the hope of enhancing one's own moral worth by comparisons with the (supposed) lesser moral status of others. The motive that is central to judgmentalism is a kind of moral one-upmanship. The judgmental person finds satisfaction in seeing others fail *because* he thinks this shows him to be better than they are. Christians who spend inordinate time examining how others are living their lives and do so in order to feel morally superior *are* judgmental. This should stop. But the mere fact of having high ideals does not constitute judgmentalism. From the perspective of many outside the church, Christians look not just judgmental but also like people giving verbal assent to life-denying rules that no human being can live by without distortion and pain. If Christians want to bear witness to the livability of covenantal sexuality, we need to do so with our lives and not with diatribes. We need to do our best to live with sexual integrity and admit when we ourselves struggle to live in accord with our ideals.

Donna Freitas's research on the relationship between religion and sexuality raises pertinent issues about sexual integrity. Her book *Sex and the Soul: Juggling Sexuality, Spirituality, Romance, and Religion on America's College Campuses* examines emerging adults' beliefs, attitudes and behaviors at three different kinds of U.S. institutions: public universities, Catholic colleges and universities, and Protestant evangelical colleges. Freitas found a basic cultural divide between two types of students: those who saw an intimate connection between religion and sex and those who split sex and religion into two entirely separate spheres. Perhaps somewhat confusingly, she calls those who integrate their religious views with their perspectives on sexuality "godly" and those who do not "secular," even though many who saw no connection between sex and religion identified themselves as Protestant, Catholic or Jewish.

Almost all of the students Freitas interviewed who fell into that "godly" group—those who not only espoused but also strove to live out a covenantal view of sexuality—were evangelical Protestants attending evangelical institutions of higher education. Freitas found almost no integration of sexuality and religion among students who attended schools that had a sharp divide between the classroom, residential life and campus ministry organizations. Students who came to such schools from backgrounds that officially espoused a covenantal view of sexuality almost always ended up participating in the campus "hookup" culture rife with casual sexual encounters. In contrast, Freitas found frequent integration of sexuality and religion at schools where the covenantal view was communicated inside and outside the classroom and enforced both by campus rules and peer attitudes. So, one positive lesson coming from Freitas's research is that only a holistic approach to inculcating sexual attitudes is likely to be effective.

But another lesson from Freitas's project is that the emerging adults she interviewed, whether they were in her "godly" or "secular" group, suffered from many sexual muddles. Few of the students that Freitas interviewed had a very mature or realistic view of human character development. Those striving to live out the covenantal view clung tightly and fearfully to a fragile "purity" that they viewed as under constant threat. Purity was something they thought they had until they "lost" it by breaking a rule for chaste conduct. On the other hand, the students who compartmentalized their religious views and their sexual behavior and who enthusiastically (or grudgingly) participated in the hookup culture showed little awareness of when they were using others or being used by them.

The "secular" students often participated in sexual activity that they would rather have avoided, but that they felt they had no basis for declining. Some participated in the campus hookup culture because they liked it, but many felt pressure to participate. All sorts of status considerations were at stake: the status of whom one hooked up with (one's partner's attractiveness or social prestige), as well as the number of hookups. Young males were self-conscious if they had too hard a time hooking up. Young females often felt like they were in a fragile situation of losing status if they hooked up too often or too easily (because they might be labeled "easy" or a "dirty girl"). On the other hand, they felt like being unwilling or unable to hook up risked their being labeled a social loser.

Freitas notes that although those striving to live out a covenantal view benefited from having boundaries and standards, their boundaries were very brittle. Freitas says, "Several young women told me that, once they lost their virginity, they felt as though they might as well continue [to be sexually active]. After all, once you've done it, what's the point of stopping?"[3] While some could call upon the resources that the Christian tradition offers for redemption and forgiveness, others experienced a redefinition of themselves as "dirty" and alienated from both God and their Christian community. She observes, "The evangelical students I interviewed who had sex were torn up about it, hating themselves for falling into it and hating sex because they thought it a wrong thing to do outside marriage."[4]

We should not be surprised to find that eighteen- to twenty-two-year-olds lack a mature view of sexuality. For the Christian, sexual maturity is one among many aspects of spiritual maturity, or Christlikeness. Sexual maturity is not a mere matter of biological or even psychophysical readiness to engage in sexual intercourse, nor is it an ability to "follow the rules." Sexual maturity is intertwined with human wholeness—with integrity. And spiritual maturity is not a destination at which we arrive early in our lives—it is a calling that is out in front of us our whole lives long.

Reflecting on Donna Freitas's student interviews should remind us that the covenantal view of sexuality can be an ideal that aids us in setting a trajectory toward sexual maturity, but if misconstrued it can hamper that development. Ideals are, in a sense, fictions, because they are never perfectly exemplified. Yet they are useful fictions. If we use ideals constructively they can serve as compass points in charting the course of our lives. Illusions are fictions too, but instead of helping us live purposefully, they bedevil us, suck us in and disable us from living well. Sexual insight involves the ability to discern the difference between ideal and illusion. It is easy for us to see the illusions embedded in the hookup culture's cocktail of pleasure and power. But the covenantal view can itself easily deteriorate from an ideal to an illusion if our commitment to it interferes with either self-knowledge or compassion toward others. This is the sort of thing Jesus warns us against in imploring us to take the beam out of our own eye before we focus on the speck in someone else's.

Those of us who adhere to the covenantal view of sexuality are, of course, aware that there are other competing views of sexuality within our culture. Altogether, I'll be setting out six conceptions of sexuality that are widely exemplified in our culture. In addition to the covenantal view, there is what I will call the procreative view (taken by traditional Roman Catholics) and the romantic, expressive, power, and plain sex views of sexuality espoused by various secular voices within our society.

The long, complex, intertwining and sometimes warring histories of these views of sexuality in Western culture have embedded these views into our ways of seeing and being, whether we are conscious of them or not. Often in this book I'll be using the words *view* and *lens* interchangeably. When philosophers and others use the term *view*, they often mean a theory. This is not a coincidence. The Greek word *theoria*, from which we get our word *theory*, was originally used of spectators in the tiered seats at a festival—those who were taking it all in, getting the big picture. People sometimes emphasize their sense that all our views should cohere into one overarching theory by talking of "worldviews." The language of worldview assumes that we can articulate what our big-picture framework theories are and see how our specific views follow from our fundamental assumptions. "Worldview talk" uses a term in which *view* is embedded, but at bottom such talk is about *theories*, where theories are often presented as being more like deductive systems than perceptions. The treatise is the appropriate genre for presenting worldviews. In discussing views of sexuality in this essay, I will be using the term *lens* more often than *theory* and leaning hard on this metaphor. Talk of *lenses* acknowledges that we might have clarity in one area and be clueless elsewhere, that our perceptions of sexuality might not be amenable to systemization, that our insights might be fragmentary but still valuable.

Often theologians and philosophers who ponder sexuality focus on defending their favored theory against rival views, implying that it constitutes the whole truth about sex. Often rival accounts of sexuality are played off against one another in a way that draws attention to the positive aspects of one account while ignoring its deficiencies, at the same time concentrating on the negative aspects of competing views. This approach is a cheap and easy way of making a preferred option look like an uncontested winner.

If we treat views as theories or systematic accounts, we weigh their pros and cons, debate, defend our favorite, pick the winner. There is a place for weighing reasons and assessing rival views— we'll be doing a considerable amount of that. Weighing reasons yields one kind of insight. But there is also a place for cultivating sensitivity to the varied ways that sexuality is viewed, for exploring how these perspectives converge and diverge.

Among Christians, our churches have taught us that the views that compete with the covenantal view are distortions caused by sin and lust—that we need to protect ourselves psychologically and spiritually from them. There is an element of truth in this claim. However, clinging too tightly to this partial truth will disable our ability to see other people and (especially) ourselves clearly. I will be discussing how the alternative lenses to the covenantal lens can supplement it and deepen the insight it provides when covenant is the central element focusing our sexual energies. We Christians too often forget that what theologians call "common grace" can undergird wisdom from non-Christian sources (Augustine called this "Egyptian gold," an allusion to the plundering of Egypt that accompanied the Israelites' exodus from bondage). We also too often forget that the continuing temporal effects of sin in the lives of Christians cause us all to be prone to distorted understanding of Christian truths. We need to ask ourselves how such distortions may have affected our grasp of covenantal sexuality.

To increase sexual insight we need to become both more self-reflective and more honest. Our lives as sexual beings are, in fact, irreducibly complex. Sex can matter to us in multiple ways. Few of us see sex through only one perspective, only one lens. Sometimes this is a curse, a major source of sexual muddle. But as we shall see, deftly combining multiple lenses can give us depth perception. There is some truth in seeing the covenantal and procreative views as "Christian," and the romantic, power, expressive and plain sex views that I'll be describing as "secular." But Christians should not unreflectively dismiss the four "secular" views as merely clouding our vision (much more will be said about this, especially in chapter two). We need to become more aware of the lenses through which we and others are viewing sexuality, concentrating on our own eyes, lenses and blind spots before presuming to diagnose others.

It is in this spirit that I have refrained from discussing issues that can, for many Christians, seem to concern "them" rather than "us" until later in the book. Examinations of casual sex, prostitution and pornography will be deferred until chapters six and seven. We will be putting first things first by introducing the lenses in the first chapter, which constitutes part one, "Basic Equipment." In the remainder of the book, then, we will be applying this basic equipment to three broad topics: Christian ideals (part one), complications (part two) and convolutions (part three).

In the two chapters that make up part two, "Christian Ideals," we will be applying the lenses to marital sexuality and sexuality in singleness. Christians, especially Protestants who lack a space for celibacy as a role-related sacred calling within the church, have seen marriage as the normative context for sexuality. After discussing marriage, we will be clarifying the differences among virginity, chastity and sexual restraint, as well as exploring the role of the virtue of chastity for both those who are single and those who are married. Along the way, we will be exploring how lenses other than the covenantal lens are deployed in the history of Christian conceptions of marriage and singleness. We will be asking whether these other lenses can supplement the covenantal view without distorting it.

Part three, "Complications," focuses on areas of sexuality where clarity can be especially hard to come by. The first chapter in this section, chapter four, addresses issues that have not gotten the ethical attention warranted by their complexity: the nature of flirtation and seduction, along with issues surrounding when wakening another's sexual interest is problematic. Chapter five takes on a complex of issues surrounding homosexuality.

In part four, "Convolutions," we will be taking a careful look at how our culture has been shaped by conceptions of sexuality that differ starkly from covenant ideals. From a covenant perspective these visions of sexuality are sadly deficient and lead to impoverished sexual lives. Chapter six looks at casual sex, and chapter seven examines the commoditization of sexuality in pornography and prostitution.

As we explore these topics together, you will be increasing your ability to discern when you are guided by an ideal and when you are befuddled by an illusion. To aid your quest for sexual insight and integrity, I will be discussing the six sexual lenses within a broad context of what is known as "Virtue Ethics." A focus on virtue puts primary emphasis on the question "What sort of person should I be or become?" The virtue approach does not neglect the question of what we should do in particular circumstances. However, it sees that *right actions* are a natural outgrowth of *being the best sort of person.* To become the best sort of person, valuable character traits like honesty, courage, fair-mindedness, generosity, self-discipline and even-temperedness are to be cultivated. Damaging character traits like cruelty, laziness, dishonesty and cowardice are to be avoided. In chapter three, I'll be explaining why the virtue of chastity, rightly understood as sexual integrity, is a central virtue. I will explain how chastity helps those who have it thrive as physical and spiritual beings. In the book's conclusion I show how chastity is aided in the quest for sexual integrity by other virtues: justice, compassion, gratitude, creativity, playfulness and reverence.

An understanding of virtue is aided by stories that show us how to succeed in our quest for our ideals. Yet often the stories that help us most are not success stories but cautionary tales that show us the dangers of less than virtuous character. I've included many stories in this book—some of them are about successfully approximating ideals, but many of them have to do with illusion. Looking squarely enough at the damage caused by sexual illusions will help clear the way for celebrating the appropriate role of sexuality in our lives.

After finishing the book, you will not have all your questions about sexuality answered, but you will be more aware of the lenses through which you and others are seeing sex. Most importantly, you'll be immunized against two illusions that plague our society: the illusion that we can see sex through no lens at all, and the illusion that sex can be our savior. I hope that this book aids your quest for sexual integrity. This is a worthy quest. To the extent that our lives are lived with sexual integrity, our sexuality will be a source of joy and delight for us and all those who are affected by it.

PART ONE

Basic Equipment

SIX SEXUAL LENSES

Sex has many meanings. This is not a recent or postmodern observation. In the biblical book Song of Solomon, we hear Hebrew voices intertwined in intricate ways to display the complexities of sexual desire and courtship. These voices sing of exuberant celebration of the body, of longing, of quest, of doubt, of loss, and of warning: on the one hand, "be drunk with love" (Song of Solomon 5:1); on the other hand, "do not stir up or awaken love until it is ready!" (Song of Solomon 8:4). For centuries within the Christian tradition, Song of Solomon was interpreted solely as a spiritual allegory. God's intention, it was thought, could not be to spend a whole biblical book singing about sex and sensuality. God's intent must have been a prefiguring of Christ's relationship to the church. Both the presence of the book in the canon and the history of the debate about its significance speak volumes to the variety of ways that sex has been viewed in Jewish and Christian traditions.

The Hebrews were not the only ancient civilization to ruminate about the meaning of sex. In ancient Greece, the great philosopher Plato recounted speeches about sexual desire in his *Symposium*. The *Symposium* is the story of a drinking party where the customary competition—seeing who can outdrink the others—is replaced with a different contest: seeing who can make the best speech in honor of Eros. *Eros* is the Greek word for sexual desire and also the name of one of the beings in the Greek mythic collection of deities. One speaker at Plato's drinking party claims that Eros is an ancient god. Others disagree, claiming that eros is a common hunger. The stuffy doctor at the party claims that eros makes the world spin. Aristophanes, the playwright, spins a tale about eros being the desire to be glued to our long-lost other half. Finally, Socrates (Plato's teacher and spokesperson) claims that eros, rightly pursued, leads beyond the physical to loving contemplation of the eternal.

The *Symposium* has an ambiguous ending. Before the speechmakers can engage the question of whether any of them have more sexual insight than the others, Plato has Alcibiades barge into the party and declare his unrequited desire to become Socrates' lover. Plato uses this dramatic device to leave picking the winner of the speechmaking contest up to his readers. Readers of the *Symposium* are still debating who within the dialogue spoke with the most wisdom.

Since ancient times, then, we have known that sex has many meanings. We have puzzled over how to view our sexuality and live it out with integrity. Philosophers, theologians, psychologists and other experts who write about sexuality can seem to be assuming their own flawless, completely objective sexual insight. But sexuality is an area where complete objectivity is very unlikely. The apostle Paul tells us in his first letter to the Corinthians that "we see through a glass, darkly" (1 Corinthians 13:12 KJV). This is true of all areas central to our humanity and spirituality. Yet we need to strive for insight, starting where we are, doing the best we can, relying on God's grace.

OPTICS AS METAPHOR

For years now, my optometrist has been swinging a machine in front of my face that looks like a clumsily rendered butterfly with two massive, thick wings. There are dials and numbers on the wings and a glass hole in each. Again and again I've been told to rest my chin on the indentation provided and look through the eyeholes.

"What is that thing called?" I finally asked. The response sounded like "foropter"—maybe this was an echo of *Lepidoptera*, the Latin term for the order of butterflies. Did its inventors intend it to look like an iron butterfly?

"P. H. O. R. O. P. T. E. R." My optometrist spelled it out for me. "Phoropter. I use it to calculate refractions."

For those of you who have not gone through the ritual of a professional eye examination, you need to know that as the lenses are rotated and dropped into place, vision gets blurrier before it gets better. An oft-repeated question is "Is it clearer now?" Multiplicity without convergence fogs our vision; multiplicity with convergence yields clarity. "Which is clearer for you? This one? Or this second one?" the optometrist asks as he or she turns dials and flips lenses. "I'm not sure," I often have to say honestly. Then the optometrist tries something new or circles around from some other direction in order to disambiguate the ambiguous.

Phoropter has a Greek root—*phore,* meaning bearing or carrying. When the lines of light refraction are carried to the optimal place at the back of both eyeballs, objects are seen with clear binocular depth perception. We call this 20/20 vision. The technical term for this is *orthophoria*—correct or optimal carrying of the light so that convergence yields clear vision.

Optics provides a useful metaphor for the quest for sexual insight. If views about sex are doctrines or theories, insight requires orthodoxy. Orthodoxy is too often assumed to preclude multiplicity. If views are lenses, however, sexual insight is aided by intellectual and moral orthophoria. In optical orthophoria, multiplicity plus convergence yields clarity. I invite you to spend the brief span of this book pondering what sexual orthophoria might entail and seeing whether you think you are closer to it by the book's end.

Optics is a useful metaphor, but not a useful allegory. Metaphors are different from allegories. In an allegory, every element within the image or story has some correspondence to the phenomena that are supposedly being illuminated. If I were using optics as an allegory, I would owe you answers to questions like: Given that some people are nearsighted and others are farsighted, how does that fact apply to deviations from sexual insight? Given that different people need different corrective prescriptions, are you advocating relativism or individualized sexual morality? What role do the moral equivalents of glaucoma and cataracts play? These are not useful questions. Take the metaphor for what it is, valuable only if not warped into an allegory.

SIX LENSES FOR VIEWING SEXUALITY

I do not have a "sexual phoropter." I do not know where to order one. I do not have kits to sell you so you can make your own. But what I do have are six "lenses" to set before you that I've observed people using in viewing sexuality. As we look together at these lenses, see how they are often combined and presupposed as people act, react and debate; and pay attention to when clarity emerges—which may not be as soon or as often as you would like.

The covenantal view. I've already given a brief summary of the covenantal view in the introduction and will be saying considerably more about it in the next chapter. For the covenantal view, sexual intercourse is more than a physical act; it is resonant of symbolism that dictates marriage as the only appropriate context for it. "Becoming one flesh" in a mystical, life-uniting sense, is an inseparable part of sexual intercourse. The union of husband and wife is seen as a mystery analogous to the union of Christ with the church. Sexual intercourse, on this view, should be an embodiment of a solemn pledge made at the marriage ceremony. To take sex lightly is not just disloyal to one's spouse but is also an affront to God. This is why the traditional wedding ceremony contains the words, "What God has joined together, let no man put asunder."

The covenantal view and what I will call the procreative view have been the most prominent views of sexuality among Christian ethicists. Both the covenantal and procreative views hold that sex is "a privileged form of self-giving between spouses that both expresses and fosters their communion of love."[1]

The procreative view. The procreative view is the official position concerning sexuality of the Roman Catholic Church, while the covenantal view is the position most often articulated in official statements on sexuality issued by Protestant denominations. These labels—covenantal and procreative—are about centers of gravity. Catholics also value the covenant of marriage and Protestants also value the generativity of sexuality. But these labels highlight major divides between official positions of Protestants and Catholics on, for example, contraception. The official teaching of the Roman Catholic Church is that artificial means of birth control distort sexual relations and should be foregone, even within marriages that have already produced numerous children. In contrast, Protestant Christians have, for the most part, not discouraged the use of birth control as a means of family planning within marriage.

Issue is at the center of the visual field of the procreative lens. Not issue in the sense of controversy or debate but issue in the sense of what flows out of sexual relations. The procreative lens sees sex's purpose as *to issue forth, to produce.* Offspring are the point of sexual encounter. The procreative view holds that actions that are fully, wholesomely sexual must be open to generativity. Thus, to be complete, sex must be heterosexual and genital and embrace the hope of fruitfulness.

The procreative view sees large parts of the delight and glory of each sexual embrace lodged in the future, in the joys of pregnancy and parenthood, the hoped-for issues of this union. "Large parts" because the procreative view of sex aspires to be *binocular*—acknowledging that wholesome sex is life-uniting (present delight) and procreative (future delight) in equal parts at the same time. The procreative view acknowledges that sexual relations that lack present delight hamper the bond between the couple no matter how fruitful they are in issuing offspring. Yet hoped-for children are acknowledged as central to marriage by traditional Catholic wedding liturgies in ways that are absent from most Protestant ceremonies.

I see six prominent views of sexuality in our culture. The romantic view, the plain sex view, the power view, and the expressive view are "secular" competitors to the procreative and covenantal views. These four secular views contrast in various important ways with the procreative and covenantal views' emphasis on marriage as the appropriate context for flourishing sexual expression.

The romantic view. In spite of the distinctions between the two "Christian" views and the four "secular" views, many see the romantic view as having significant common ground with the procreative and covenantal views. One element of common ground is that those who hold the romantic view often talk in terms of sex as sacred and as a gift to be preserved to be given to someone of profound significance.

The romantic view holds that sexual expression should be reserved for when you have found someone with whom you are deeply in love and who loves you in return. The romantic view is sensitive to a distinction between lust, which is sexual desire divorced from the goal of interpersonal intimacy, and erotic love, which is a way of valuing another person intensely and holistically. While passing feelings of lust may often be beyond our control, the romantic view disapproves of lust as a habit. Habitual lusting routinely gives way to sexual desire divorced from any personal relation with the object of one's desire. In contrast, the romantic view holds that sex should be connected with a thirst for deep psychological and bodily knowledge. Mutually reciprocated gift-giving and intimacy are the purpose of sexuality.

The romantic lens sees sexual intercourse as the appropriate consummation of romantic anticipation. The feeling of being in love is a feeling that one's beloved is an irreplaceable soul mate. Based on this perceived irreplaceability, the romantic view might be taken to hold that the sexual bond is naturally exclusive. Romantic feelings set the love relationship apart from all others.[2]

Complications arise, however, when romantic feelings do not last or when someone who has made a commitment to sexual exclusivity finds himself or herself in love with someone else. For example, philosopher Richard Taylor, in his book *Having Love Affairs,* uses the romantic view to underwrite his claim that "the joys of illicit and passionate love, which include but go far beyond the mere joys of sex, are incomparably good."[3] While finding fault with Taylor's pro-love-affair arguments, philosopher Mike W. Martin makes milder, but related, claims. Martin argues that in cases where erotic love has died within a marriage and one of the spouses has fallen in love with someone else, love-inspired adultery may not be immoral. Martin asserts that in an ideal world, marriages that have become loveless would be ended cleanly, before new relationships begin. But, Martin asserts, "at least sometimes there may be good reasons for pursuing alternative relationships before officially ending a bad marriage."[4]

The romantic view emphasizes interpersonal intimacy, but sees the duration of commitment as contingent. Commitment lasts for as long as romantic love lasts.

But commitment is important. A one-time sexual encounter with a stranger may be consensual sex, but it is not an appropriate use of sexuality on the romantic view. For the romantic view, even being a "considerate lover" is not enough if all that means is seeking to give sexual satisfaction within uncommitted sexual encounters. Yet in practice the romantic view often leads to serial monogamy because the commitment embraced by the romantic view is rooted in intense feelings that may or may not be sustainable in any given relationship.

So there is a major contrast between the procreative and covenantal views on the one hand, and the romantic view on the other, about issues of whether love-inspired premarital or extramarital sex is ever appropriate. Still, the romantic view shares a disapproval of casual sex with the procreative and covenantal views. This is a major contrast between the romantic view and what I will call the "plain sex view."

The plain sex view. The label "plain sex view" comes from an article entitled "Plain Sex" written by U.S. philosopher Alan Goldman in the 1970s.[5] Goldman speaks for those for whom the advent of reliable and convenient contraception in the twentieth century undermined any link between sex and commitment. From the point of view of interpersonal interaction and behavior, procreation was seen as a biological byproduct of sexuality—a byproduct that could be and should be controlled at will. With the practice of "safe sex," recreational sex began to seem appropriate between consenting adults. Throughout human history some people had, of course, seen sex as mainly about pleasure, but before reliable contraception such people were widely viewed as irresponsible—libertines and gigolos, if male, and something even more impolite, if female.

From a plain sex point of view, the link among love, commitment and sex was a cultural construction that grew up in a context where the procreative consequences of sexuality meant that sex should be confined to marriage, so that resulting children could be raised by their biological parents. Once it became technologically possible to easily block the reproductive consequences of sexual intercourse, Goldman and others asked, "Cannot sex be acknowledged as just plain sex—as something valuable and desirable for itself?" This view claims that cultural construct that linked love and sex are outmoded. The plain sex view posits that sexuality is now best seen as simply an acute physical desire for an intensely pleasurable physical activity that naturally leads to engaging in bodily exploration and intensely pleasurable activity.

More recently philosopher Igor Primoratz gives what he takes to be a friendly characterization of the plain sex view: "Other things being equal, it is better to be able to enjoy both loving and loveless sex than only the former. A person who enjoyed sex as part of loving relationships but was completely incapable of enjoying casual sex would seem to be missing out on something."[6] Movies, novels and advertisements routinely depict characters that hold this view, which has become commonplace in many parts of contemporary Western culture.[7]

Despite its name, even the plain sex view is not just a neutral description of what sex and sexuality are. It and the other five views each entail contrasting recommendations about how we *should* comport ourselves as sexual beings regardless of how we actually behave. When evaluating sex, the plain sex view puts its emphasis on mutual consent and mutual consideration leading to mutual sexual satisfaction. When "no one gets hurt" and each party gets what he or she wants, plain sex appears to avoid lots of problems.

The power view. The power view of sexuality contrasts with the plain sex view in emphasizing the significance of sex. The power view acknowledges sexuality as *energy,* as a *force.* Beyond this, the power lens sees interpersonal power dynamics as so deeply entrenched in our sexuality that sex is *never* just about pleasure. Sexual desire and sexual activity heighten our awareness both of our powers as erotic beings and of our profound vulnerability. Sexual interaction lays us bare and can strip us of control as we surrender to desire. Yet sexuality also is a potent instrument for controlling others. Knowing oneself as a being who can command another's sexual attention is invigorating. Experiencing oneself as sexually attractive is enlivening. Yet this power is also fragile and puts one at the mercy of another's gaze—another person's way of seeing. When I become a "sex object," someone else decides whether I am valued or set aside, desired or dismissed.

One characterization that twentieth-century French philosopher Jean Paul Sartre gives of sexual dynamics is largely a matter of preemptive objectification. In order to seize control and not be controlled, I need to objectify my sexual "partner" (in thought or by actions) before my sexual "partner" can objectify me. "Partner" becomes a misnomer because the mutuality of such encounters is mutual rivalry in a contest over power.

The power dynamics inherent in sexuality are, at their darkest, the root of the link between sex and violence. This link is, in turn, the source of some vulgar slang expressions that do double duty. In some contexts these words mean "to have sexual intercourse" ("Come on, baby, let's _____.") and in other contexts they mean "to damage or denigrate" ("_____ you!"). Although the link between sex and violence is often covert, rape, sexual assault and the sexual exploitation of children are obvious forms of sexual violence; these are sex-as-power in its rawest form.

The link between sex and power is often convoluted. Consider, for example, an image from a cover of the U.S. magazine *Rolling Stone* that was seen to have enough iconic significance to be included in a book on contemporary art. The three female members of the rock group Destiny's Child, dressed in skimpy halter tops and hot pants made of military camouflage material, stand with legs spread, engaging the viewer with a sexually provocative gaze. The combat boots and ammo belts seem to show these women as empowered—perhaps as dominatrixes. The subtitle of the cover article is "A Story of Discipline and Desire," emphasizing the drive that has made these women famous. But the social subtext—that they are sexually available to the presupposed male viewer of the image—is reinforced by the pun "Booty Camp!" printed in large letters in front of their sculpted abdomens. Who exactly is empowered by such images—those depicted, those viewing the images, or those using the images to promote ideas and products in our consumer society? Who is harmed or exploited by these images?

The main recommendation coming out of the power view is self-protection. Since sex and power are a potent and murky mix, one must enter into sexual relationships with one's eyes wide open, savvy about the potential for exploitation and manipulation, taking care to preserve one's own dignity by not being the victim of another's conscious or unconscious exertions of power.

The expressive view. While the power view of sexuality emphasizes the interpersonal power dynamics in sexual interaction, the expressive view focuses on the role of sexuality within personal development. Sexual expression garners creative power. Seen through the expressive lens, sex appears *empowering* without being an exertion of power *over* another or at the expense of another. This emphasis on sexuality as a source of personal empowerment that can and should be deployed without hampering the empowerment of others sets the expressive view apart from the power view of sex. Writer Sally Tinsdale voices a modest version of the expressive view when she asserts, "Sex can help us to like ourselves and find a generosity of spirit, open ourselves to the world and simply be alive."[8] Theologian Carter Heyward's summary of the expressive view is more emphatic and expansive: "I believe that the celebration of the erotic and of our desire to express it sexually *ought* to be a major issue in our life together because it is the primary wellspring of our capacity to be creative together—to love one another, write poetry, struggle for justice and friendship."[9]

Philosopher Robert Solomon has set forth the most literal version of the expressive view of sexuality. He calls sexual activity "body language" and sees identifiable expressive physical gestures as the bodily equivalent of sentences. Solomon explicitly distances his expressive view of sexuality from the romantic view by asserting that "love, it seems, is not best expressed sexually, for its sexual expression is indistinguishable from other attitudes." In contrast, he thinks that tenderness, domination, trust, possessiveness, submissiveness and conflict are vividly conveyed through the gestures of body language.[10]

Because the expressive lens sees sexual expression as vital to personal empowerment, it sees sexual restraint as diminishing or warping the self. Sigmund Freud's assertion that most people are not capable of abstinence, and his graphic case studies in the consequences of sexual repression, can be seen as embedded in the expressive view. The importance placed on sexual expression as part of a full human life sets the view apart from the plain sex view. In contrast to the plain sex view, the expressive view sees sexuality as something much more than a desire for pleasure, however intense. It sees sexuality and sexual activity as central to our identity. To forego sex would, if Solomon is right, be like foregoing writing or speech and, if Freud is right, be inviting neurosis.

SEEING THROUGH THE SIX LENSES

So these are the six sexual lenses that we will be working with in this book: procreative, covenantal, romantic, plain sex, power and expressive. Each lens, when taken as the sole or central organizing principle, will see the world of sexuality very differently, including the history of alternative conceptions of sexuality itself. From a covenantal view, the creational intention for sexuality has been, from the very beginning, lifelong bonding between spouses. In contrast, from a plain sex view, marriage is a somewhat late invention among human cultures imposed on the quest for sexual pleasure in order to civilize the sexual impulse and domesticate it within marriage for the sake of social order. Sexual

Table 1. Six Sexual Lenses

Covenantal Lens: Sexual intercourse forges a permanent bond between two people that is intended as a representation of God's covenantal relationship with God's people. Sexual intercourse is a life-uniting act that should only occur within marriage.
Procreative Lens: The goal or purpose of human sexuality is reproduction. Non-reproductive uses of sexuality are misuses of sexuality, because they divide the reproductive purpose of sexuality from its unifying function.
Romantic Lens: Sexual intercourse is the appropriate expression of a particular sort of deep emotional attachment (romantic love) with one's beloved. Loveless sex is inappropriate. People should be sexually faithful as long as love lasts.
Plain Sex Lens: Sexual desire is an acute bodily desire for physical contact with the body of another. Sex is an intensely pleasurable physical activity. Sex should be based on mutual consent leading to mutual sexual satisfaction, so that "no one gets hurt."
Power Lens: Sexuality is a potent instrument for controlling others. Sexual desire is the desire to possess another, while wanting to avoid being objectified by the other. One must be savvy about the potential for sexual exploitation, manipulation and violence.
Expressive Lens: Sex is a source of personal empowerment that is central to human flourishing. Sexual restraint is unnatural, yet sexuality should be deployed without hampering the empowerment of others.

lenses are so pervasive in their influence that there is no perspective-neutral ground from which to tell the story of the development of the lenses.

The search for clarity in these matters, and for sexual insight, brings us around again to the desire for a sexual phoropter. Literal phoropters like the one my optometrist uses are extremely complicated, having three rotating discs containing lenses. Some of the lenses are convex, curving outward. Others are concave. This makes a difference in how they bend the light. These lenses can be dropped into place in different combinations and can also be rotated. As the optometrist changes the combinations of lenses, the

clarity of what is seen through the phoropter increases or de-
creases. The optometrist takes careful notes on the effects of all
these variables, with the goal of closing in on just the right prescription—the prescription that yields orthophoria, or 20/20 vision. The contrast term for *orthophoria* is *heterophoria*—light fails
to converge where and when it should and we end up with blurred
vision. Multiplicity without convergence results in heterophoria.

Unless you have some professional interest in optics, you spend
a lot more time looking *through* lenses than looking at them. Looking directly at a lens—optical or metaphorical—soon exhausts our
interest. These preliminary sketches of the six views of sexuality
are thinnish and flatish. To really begin to "see" the sexual lenses,
we are best served by deploying them and looking through them to
see what sex looks like when they are in use. We can get some practice with these sexual lenses I've introduced by using them to diagnose a particular case of heterophoria. This case is an article that
appeared in the widely respected U.S. news magazine *Newsweek*.

The article, "The Myths of Teen Sex," contains this claim: "Most
teens who had oral sex were having intercourse, and only one in
four teen virgins had oral sex—not exactly the markings of a teen
oral sex epidemic."[11] The article's stated goal is to combat "hysteria" over the current sexual practices among teenagers.

But this claim about oral sex seems muddled. No matter how
large the overlap is between teens having oral sex and teens having intercourse, the overlap cannot count as evidence against an
oral sex "epidemic." Epidemics are about frequency and swiftness
of spread. Why would those who are concerned about teens having oral sex be less "hysterical" if they knew that they were also
having intercourse?

"Teen sexual behavior in general hasn't changed much since
1991" is another claim in this article. This at least is evidence
that even if there is a teen oral sex epidemic, it's not gaining
momentum.

The "myth" that "The Myths of Teen Sex" seeks to expose is that teens, either because of former U.S. President Bill Clinton's example or in like-mindedness with him, don't think that oral sex counts as sex. Once teens tumble to this "insight," so the so-called myth goes, oral sex spreads like wildfire. Teens would flock to oral sex as a way of getting intense pleasure without having sex ("while remaining chaste" is how the article puts it). If 75 percent of teens who are having oral sex are also having intercourse, then they are not using oral sex as a substitute for intercourse. And if the frequency of oral sex among teens hasn't increased since before the Clinton/Lewinsky scandal, teen behavior hasn't been influenced by social changes precipitated by news coverage of the scandal.

In its larger context, the logic of the article seems to improve. Or does it? How many parents of a teen would be less worried knowing that if a teen is having oral sex, he or she is very likely also having intercourse?

"Only one in four teen *virgins* had oral sex." Let's ponder this a moment. If oral sex is compatible with virginity, why did so many people in the U.S. snicker at Clinton's claim, "I did not have sex with that woman Monica Lewinsky"? Who believes that oral sex isn't really sex? Does anyone, teen or adult, believe that oral sex is a way "kids could satisfy their sexual urges while remaining chaste"? At some level, the author of this article appears to both see things this way and not see things this way. That's muddled.

The fact is that a kind of muddled double vision is embedded in the *American Heritage Dictionary* definition of *virgin*. *Virgin* means one who has not experienced sexual intercourse. But *virgin* also means someone (usually a girl or woman) who is chaste. Oral sex is not intercourse, so it would seem that a virgin can engage in oral sex without ceasing to be a virgin. But is oral sex a chaste activity? If not, then the second dictionary characterization makes oral sex incompatible with virginity. Americans smirked over Bill Clinton's "That depends on what 'is' is" when he was interrogated about whether he had lied in denying having had sex with Lewinsky. Would we, or should we, still have laughed if he had said, "That depends on what 'sex' is"?

Equivocations and muddle are written into the language we use about sex and are hard to avoid even among professional writers who are taking great care. *Newsweek* is not a sloppy magazine. Many would see Bill Clinton's "Monica Affair" as breathtakingly foolish, but Clinton's assertion that he did not lie when he denied having had sex with Monica has a basis in standard uses of English.

Remarks in "The Myths of Teen Sexuality" are examples of how we frequently see the world through multiple understandings of sexuality without even realizing it. This particular article flips through at least three different understandings of sexuality. It does this unreflectively and unselfconsciously.

Look carefully again at the short phrase "only one in four teen virgins had oral sex." Here the author looks through two different sexual lenses at the same time in a divergent way. The conceptual connection between virginity and having refrained from intercourse has its home in the procreative view of sex. For the procreative view, sex means heterosexual copulation—this is normal and normative for this view. But the procreative view would never say "only one in four . . . had oral sex" in a calm, dismissive way. This "only" comes from the plain sex view's perspective—a view that takes sex to be mainly about pleasure.

There is a third perspective in the article, seemingly invisible to the author when she is focusing on the study results she's discussing instead of on her article's opening images. The article opens with stories of boys lined up along walls and girls down on their knees. Stories of boys competing to see who can receive oral sex from the most girls. These scenarios are about sex through the power lens—about some people exerting power, about others going along with the game. Concern about abuses of power that rob young people of their dignity is not "hysteria," nor should it be "cured" by statistics. The article concludes with a flippant and dismissive reassurance: "For every birthday party where the boys line up against the wall, there are plenty more where the kids drink too much soda, play [the video game called] Grand Theft Auto and then simply go home." Christians, along with many humanists and certainly many feminists, hold that it is not hysteria to be concerned about teens kneeling in the service of ambiguous power dynamics, even if those kneeling constitute only a statistical minority.

This brief look at each of these six sexual lenses will help us in honing our sexual insight in the coming chapters. Rival views of how sex matters in our pluralistic society often mean that there are few shared understandings, conventions or rules of engagement. Perhaps as often as not we are all squinting at sexuality through multiple lenses in ways that give rise to internal muddle. It is little wonder that there is so much pain arising from misunderstanding and so many disappointed expectations in the sexual realm. Yet the deep joy and shared understanding that are the fruit of mature sexual mutuality are fully human aspirations.

Yet the six sexual lenses can be more than mutually exclusive rivals. As we will see, the perspectives of the multiple sexual lenses converge when the covenantal lens is taken as the central organizing lens. This brings sexuality into focus— letting us achieve some measure of sexual orthophoria and allowing the covenantal view to be enriched by what these other lenses reveal.

A Brief Aside for the Philosophically Minded

I want to include some brief remarks about the philosophical strategy that underlies this book. This section is a bit technical. Since the rest of the book can be understood without reading this section, those who are less curious about philosophical technicalities should skip directly to chapter two.

The view of ethics being presupposed in this book is roughly Aristotelian. Aristotle held that ethics is not like geometry. Philosophy is not a matter of accessing some infallible or esoteric knowledge. Deductions about what we should do cannot be derived from axioms that give us infallible access to the Good. If we want to investigate what the good life is, we need to consult human experience as it is encoded in common sense and the opinions of those respected for their wisdom. Christians who use an Aristotelian view to investigate ethical questions will grant the Bible and the best of Christian theology pride of place among "the wise," but will also acknowledge that while God's revelation is infallible, human interpretations of that revelation are limited and prone to err. Critical examination of interpretations of the Christian tradition is, thus, always appropriate.

Aristotle describes his method this way: "We must set out the appearances, and first of all go through the puzzles. In this way we must prove the common beliefs about these ways of being affected—ideally, all the common beliefs, but if not all, then most of them and the most important. For if the objections are solved, and the common beliefs are left, it will be adequate proof."[12] Aristotle scholars have labeled this the "aporetic" method (from *aporia*, the Greek word for puzzle, tangle or knot). The aporetic method has three steps: (1) assemble the data ("appearances," i.e., the opinions of the wise and of common sense); (2) identify the puzzles (i.e., look for contradictions among the opinions or difficulties and paradoxes raised by the data); (3) construct a theory that solves the puzzles while preserving the most important parts of the data. Showing that a theory can bring coherence to what looked initially like a puzzling divergence and muddle is the closest we can come within ethics to "proving" that a view contains more truth than other alternative views.

Notice that Aristotle thought we should not just take received opinion at face value, but that we cannot afford to ignore it either. Aristotle's method presupposes that a theory that flies in the face of common sense at least has to be able to explain how so many people could have been misled for so long.

The metaphor of the optometrist's phoropter is meant to give the aporetic method intuitive appeal. The goal of this book as a whole is to show that a robust, twenty-first-century covenantal view can make sense of sexuality by acknowledging the partial truths contained in the procreative, romantic, expressive, power and plain sex views of sexuality.

PART TWO

Christian Ideals—
How Christians See
and Are Seen

2

MARITAL SEXUALITY

I missed my son's wedding rehearsal, but I gained an important sexual insight that night. My in-laws, two fragile people in their eighties, had undertaken an arduous plane trip to attend their grandson's wedding. Two hours before the rehearsal was to start, my mother-in-law, Grace, fell and broke her shoulder. Since my husband was the minister who was conducting the ceremony, he absolutely needed to be at the rehearsal. So I headed off with the group of family members who took Grace to the emergency room. Once she was receiving medical attention, I rushed over to the restaurant where the rehearsal dinner was held. From then until we got my in-laws to our home at 1 a.m., my husband and I tag-teamed hospital coverage. We tried our best to do two vital things: host a joyful event for our son and his bride, and help my father-in-law, Virg, negotiate the intricacies of getting quality medical care for his wife hundreds of miles from their own doctor. We were very grateful that the next day everyone, including Grace, was able to enjoy the wedding.

How was this an occasion for sexual insight? The words that my son and daughter-in-law rehearsed that night, and pledged to one another in earnest the next day, included audacious promises.

They promised to share their lives with one another, "cleave to one another" "in sickness and in health," until death parts them.

As I watched Virg by his wife's hospital gurney, I saw the effect of decades of living those vows. This eighty-year-old man, himself far from robust, would not leave his wife's side or even eat until he knew Grace's arm was stabilized and she was comfortable. Virg held Grace's hand, watched her every reaction, winced with her pain. After sixty years of marriage, he knew her—body and soul.

THE "BODY AND SOUL" OF SEXUALITY IN MARRIAGE

Viewed through the plain sex lens, which sees sex solely as passing physical pleasure, this story has little if anything to do with sex. But seen through the covenantal lens, sex is about coming to know who someone else is, body and soul. When my husband pronounced our son and daughter-in-law husband and wife, he invoked God's blessing on their unconditional pledge of sexual fidelity—a pledge made regardless of how the future, including the future of the relationship, might go.[1] As a mother, I want the best for both of my sons and their wives. I hope for wonderful marriages for them—marriages in which they have a full and satisfying sexual relationship.

I know from experience that decades of sexual intimacy build layer upon layer of knowledge of one's spouse's body. Bodies remember. Marital sex is lovemaking that explores not just one another's bodies at particular times, but one another's embodied selves as they reach from remembered times and to anticipated times. If my sons' marriages endure, these couples will be able to call upon their intimate knowledge of one another, body and soul. This knowledge will help them to be faithful companions in health, in sickness and ultimately in death. While few couples in their twenties are focusing on such matters as they are wed, this is the aspiration that the vows they speak espouse.

This is foreshadowed in our sexuality itself. The French language beautifully reveals and celebrates this. One expression for *orgasm* in French is "the little death" ("la petite mort"). In a frank chapter in her book *I've Heard the Vultures Singing,* writer Lucia Perillo talks about how her muscular dystrophy has affected her sexuality. As part of her treatment she had a device the size of a tuna can implanted in her belly just below her waist, its outline visible under the raised skin. She reports, "When I am trying to give an erotic purpose to my nakedness and do not have an appropriate piece of drapery, I leave my hand there like Napoleon with his wrist curled into a pocket."[2]

Perillo comes to terms with how to remain sexual while chronically ill. This gives her a context of reflecting on sex as "a little death." Orgasm strips us of all decorum and, temporarily, of bodily control. Perillo reflects that many find it more romantic to close their eyes during intercourse. This shuts out the "expression of wild ferocity, or slackening" on one's partner's face. With eyes closed, you can call up a prettified fantasy to replace what "little death" looks like. Perillo finds her husband, Jim, more truly romantic. Jim could have turned away sexually from his ailing wife or closed his eyes and pretended to be making love to someone unscarred. Instead she says, "One of the most arousing memories of my recent life is Jim batting my hand away from where I was using it to anchor the hem of my T-shirt, this when the foreplay was just starting to take, him saying *I don't care if I see it.*"[3]

Such sexual maturity is not achieved overnight. In very traditional wedding services, the bride and groom say to one another "with my body, I thee worship." This "worship" that takes place on the marriage bed helps us know ourselves and our beloved as incarnate within a shared history of better and worse, sickness and health—to know one another as vulnerable, mortal flesh. Such worship can help us savor days of robust vitality; it can also prepare us for the day when the body fails and sickness and death take over. This is a gift that covenantal sex can give us. Ultimately, this is a gift of grace.

Marital Sexuality and the Six Lenses

At the heart of both the covenantal and procreative views of sexuality is fully devoted sexual intimacy, embracing the whole embodied history of another: for better, for worse; for richer, for poorer; forsaking all others. The plain sex, power and expressive views of sexuality entail no such commitments. One writer, commenting from these noncommittal points of view, disparages traditionalists about marriage as "compulsive monogomists."[4] But a tenacious trajectory of following through on one's promises is neither arbitrary nor irrational.

Marriage, seen through the plain sex, expressive and power lenses does look daft, when each of these lenses is taken in isolation from any of the other lenses. The plain sex view is rooted in the indisputable fact that most people are capable of being sexually attracted to lots of different people. In fact, those striving to live out promises of sexual exclusivity often find the profligacy of their attractions more than a little inconvenient. If sex is just about pleasure, as the plain sex view holds, then why not indulge these attractions—why make promises that limit the sources of one's sexual pleasure?

Similarly, the expressive lens can make marriage look like volunteering to truncate one's range of sexual expression, analogous to the oddity of a violinist pledging only to play with one accompanist and no other. Some radical feminists have used the power lens to critique marriage. Though not speaking for all feminists, such radical feminists have argued that monogamy is always ultimately about male power—that it is an institution founded by males with the purpose of asserting dominance over women. And many nonfeminists who view sex through the power lens also see marriage as either hemming in sexual power or as a battlefield for the war between the sexes.[5]

The romantic lens, taken on its own, makes getting married seem a proper next step after two people confirm that they are in love. When we are in love, we see our beloved as our ideal mate; we cannot imagine living without him or her. Wanting to declare our undying love for one another in a public ceremony seems absolutely natural. But romantic love doesn't always last as long as a marriage does. Thus, as we alluded to in chapter one, while the language of romance is "I will love you forever," the reality is that sometimes romance fades. While commitment seems natural to those who are in love, *unconditional* commitment seems just as irrational through the romantic lens, taken on its own, as it does through the plain sex, power and expressive lens, taken on their own. "I'll be sexually faithful to you as long as I am in love with you," would be a saner and more fitting promise for the romantic to make. As philosopher Jeffrey Weeks observes, "in the Western world . . . the stress now . . . is not so much on the qualities that make for a lifetime's sexual partnership but on the pleasures and satisfactions that can be obtained from the particular relationship—so long as it lasts. Meaning resides less in the 'ties that bind' than in the passions that unite, until they fade; then we start all over again."[6]

Given the gulf between the faithful sexuality endorsed by the covenantal and procreative lenses and the relative fickleness of the plain sex, expressive, power and romantic lens, are these four "secular" sexual lenses of any value to Christians? My answer to this question is yes. Power, expressive, romantic and plain sex are not mere rival views to marital sexuality that by marrying we effectively forsake. Because the perspectives of the multiple sexual lenses converge when the covenantal lens is taken as the central organizing lens, the six sexual lenses can be more than mutually exclusive rivals. Indeed, without what can be learned from the other lenses, the covenantal lens does not yield a full-orbed view of marital sexuality. Yet when placed at the center of our sexual vision, it can put the other five views in their proper places.

Why do I say that the covenantal lens, on its own, doesn't show us enough about marital sexuality? The covenantal view reveals the boundaries within which sexual intercourse should happen— that sex should happen within marriage. The covenantal view also tells us that husbands and wives should fulfill their "marital duties" to one another (see 1 Corinthians 7:1-5). But beyond that, the covenantal view doesn't say much about the psychophysical dynamics of how sexuality should be lived out within a marriage. As C. S. Lewis points out in *The Four Loves*, there have been historical periods in which the covenantal view was combined only with the emphasis on sex as an appetite provided by the plain sex view. Lewis notes:

> Most of our ancestors were married off in early youth to partners chosen by their parents on grounds that had nothing to do with Eros. They went to the act [of sexual intercourse] with no other "fuel," so to speak, than plain animal desire. And they did right; honest Christian husbands and wives, obeying their fathers and mothers, discharging to one another their "marriage debt," and bringing up families in the fear of the Lord.[7]

While I agree with Lewis that this was perfectly proper, I also am grateful that sexuality within my own marriage has meant a lot more than "animal passion" or marital duty.

In earlier periods in the Western world, and in a variety of other places up to the present time, marriage has been a matter of family continuity, economic necessity or social stability. Romantic attachment had little to do with marriage. Power was exercised by a paterfamilias, who kept his household, including his wife, in order. Fathers arranged their children's marriages and gave their daughters away to fitting suitors. Husbands may or may not have cared about the sexual satisfaction of their wives. Wives in many historical periods in many places around the world were presumed to put up with sex as the price of producing children and keeping their husbands content.[8] The sexual relations within these marriages were sanctioned by the marriage covenant and, as long as they were consensual and nonabusive, were morally permissible.[9] Yet the marital sex within such marriages was impoverished.

Sex is better when it is expressive of deep affection. Sex is better when it attends to the mutual pleasure of husbands and wives. Sex is better with a partner whom one deeply appreciates as a gendered embodiment of human excellence. Sex is better when it is shaped by virtues that guard against subtle but exploitive deployments of power. Sex is better when it is fecund in a timely way that blesses those called to be parents. Sex that lacks these features isn't ipso facto immoral—it's just less good.

If many Western Christians in the twenty-first century take all this for granted, this is not because all these claims are imbedded in the covenantal view of sexuality. Contemporary Christians are used to viewing sexuality through multiple lenses, whether they realize this or not. Christians in various cultural and historical settings have combined the covenantal lens with differing combinations of other lenses. Prior to the Renaissance, the link between marriage and romantic attachment was not at all common.[10] Prior even the 1970s, there wasn't a lot of discussion among Christians about the importance of sexual pleasure within marriage. But it didn't take very long after the publication of *The Joy of Sex* in 1972 for Christian authors to recognize a need for a Christian alternative to this book that illustrated the pleasures of plain sex. Now Christian marriage manuals about how to have great marital sex are widely available. What they teach about sexual technique often doesn't differ remarkably from secular alternatives; rather, the contrast lies in combining the covenantal lens with an emphasis on sexual pleasure.

We should be grateful for these historical developments. Sex that isn't pleasure-full, expressive or embedded in a romantic history is less good than sex that is because it is less supportive of marital love. Loveless marriages can be moral marriages—they can even be holy marriages—but they are nonetheless lacking in an important good appropriate to marriage. Marital love is love that enables the couple to imagine and live out each of their destinies while shaping, being shaped by, and unfolding in and with the destiny of their spouse.[11] Sex that is not just covenantal, but which also provides the proper place for pleasure, romance and procreation, nourishes marital love in ways that sex which falls short in these areas cannot. Sex that takes into account the expressive capacities of sexuality and ensures that the power dynamics of sexuality are harnessed for mutual benefit enlivens and guards marital love.

Figure 2

To see how overlapping lenses, and the relative emphasis among them, makes a difference in how we conceive of marital sexuality, it will be useful to compare the view that I am recommending with that put forward by theologian David Matzko McCarthy in his book *Sex and Love in the Home*. McCarthy says, "The true superiority of sexual intercourse in marriage is that it doesn't have to mean very much."[12] McCarthy contrasts his recommended view of Christian marital sexuality with both the commercialized view of sex found in society at large and what theologians call "personalism," which includes an account of sex as a theologically freighted "total person" encounter. The latter view, he thinks, is too beholden to romanticism, too idealistic and too individualistic to be an adequate Christian conception. McCarthy urges the importance of everyday household practices that open families to their neighborhoods and surrounding communities.[13] These include apt relationships among husband and wife and their children, as well as practices that reach out into neighborhoods and civil society. Marriages flourish when they are part of an interdependent network of households in community. McCarthy argues that good household practices embedded in flourishing communities are more important to thriving marriages than romance or significant sex.

McCarthy seeks to deromanticize marital sexuality and draw a stark contrast between covenantal sexuality and both romantic and expressive views. Instead, I am seeking to "plunder the Egyptian gold" that I perceive to be available in romantic, expressive, power and plain sex views of sexuality.

At one level, the dispute between McCarthy and me sounds like an empirical disagreement. If that were true, the way to settle the issue would be to do a sociological study. We could try to identify a group of married couples who were having romantic, expressive and pleasurable sex and another group of couples where "sex doesn't have to mean very much." We could measure the comparative intensity and durability of marital love within the two groups. Based on this we could decide whether covenantal and procreative marriages are enhanced and strengthened if they also include expressive, pleasurable and romantic sexuality or not.

On the other hand, David Matzko McCarthy may be exaggerating for rhetorical effect. He may think that, taken as a whole, the sexual history of a married couple *should be* significant—that it *should mean very much*. One way of construing his concern is that he fears the romantic lens has not just supplemented but displaced the covenantal lens among the personalists whom he criticizes. If he is exaggerating in order to emphasize this point, then what he means is both true and valuable, for an overemphasis on the romantic sexual lens can endanger marital love.

When combining the sexual lenses, putting the covenantal lens in the center transforms how sexuality is seen through the other lenses. When plain sex is brought into the orbit of covenantal sex, pleasure is still an important sexual value, but it is not the only value. Sex is no longer merely about physical desire and sensation, yet the dynamics of sexual physiology and response are not ignored. When the expressive lens is brought into the orbit of covenantal sex, the nature of the marriage covenant dictates what is appropriately expressed sexually. As we saw in chapter one, Robert Solomon thinks that tenderness, domination, trust, possessiveness, submissiveness and conflict can all be vividly conveyed sexually. But when the covenantal and expressive lenses are combined, trust and tenderness will be much more appropriate to express sexually than will anger or resentment or conflict.

THE DOMINANT COVENANTAL LENS IN CHRISTIAN MARITAL SEXUALITY

It is important to note that *which lens is dominant or central* will make a difference when various lenses are combined. Many Christians describe their view of sexuality as covenantal, but in practice have a romantic or expressive view of sexuality as their central governing paradigm. Such Christians will view being in love as a sufficient condition for legitimizing sexual intercourse and view having fallen in love with someone other than their spouse as a justification for divorce and remarriage.

But Christians for whom the covenantal lens is really central will not see having "fallen out of love" an adequate justification for divorce. New Testament scholar Richard B. Hays deplores the fact that "the church has swallowed a great quantity of pop psychology that has no foundation in the biblical depiction of marriage. . . . When the marital union is rightly understood as a *covenant*, the question of divorce assumes a very different aspect."[14] Hays criticizes a recommendation by John Shelby Spong that churches develop liturgies for blessing the dissolutions of marriages. Spong notes that many Christians are divorcing for a range of reasons, including failures to communicate or concluding that they are no longer in love. He advocates that such ceremonies would help divorced people to feel less isolated and cut off from the Christian community.[15] Here I side with Hays.

Indeed, there is much wisdom on this subject in such a secular source as Susan Cheever's frank memoir of sexual addiction, *Desire*. Cheever says, "We tell our young men and women that 'falling in love' is the basis for building a life; it is not. Falling in love is a delicious, astonishing experience, but it has very little connection to the feelings and abilities two people need in order to build a life together and sustain a family. Falling in love is a wonderful, addictive, obsessive experience that usually lasts less than twenty months."[16] Cheever found herself addicted to the dopamine rush of infatuation. As soon as the newness of the love experience wore off, she needed to move on to a new partner in order to experience the same "high." She came to realize that she was using and abusing other people as her "drug" of choice.

Christians *should* beware of the distortion caused by ceding the centrality of covenantal focus to romanticism. But this does not mean that Christians need to disparage and eschew the romantic lens altogether. We must, however, be careful to distinguish true romantic love from infatuation. In my book *The Disciplined Heart: Love, Destiny and Imagination* I argued that the Christian tradition has the conceptual resources for making this distinction. There I used the term *destiny* to denote a narrative account of the history and unfolding of those potentials that God is pleased with bringing to fruition in each particular person. I distinguished *imagination,* which is insight into someone's destiny, from *fiction-making,* which is the construction and projection of a narrative for oneself or another that is unconnected with that person's destiny. In true romantic love, imagination allows us to see our beloved as fulfilling our personal ideal of manhood or womanhood without distorting who God intends them to be. While true romantic love involves idealization, it does not involve distortion. In this way it contrasts with infatuation, because infatuation always involves fiction-making.

Marriages based on only romantic love will be fragile because they depend on the continued dovetailing of gender-based ideals with unfolding destinies. This is so whether romantic love is *true* love (yielding a truthful vision of the beloved) or is mere infatuation. My spouse may change in ways that diverge from my romantic idealization of him or her. So marriages, in order to be strong, are best constituted by a combination of marital love and romantic love, supplemented with friendship and Christian charity.

Nonetheless, those of us who have marriages where romantic love has lasted far longer than Cheever's predicted twenty months have good reason for gratitude. And even when romantic sexuality gives way early in the marriage to expressive, covenantal, procreative or plain sex, it can be enriched by being the extension of a relational history that included romantic sexuality. Perhaps the most fortunate marriages are those in which romantic sexuality is at least an episodic, if not an ever-present, aspect of the relationship.

Yet one tragedy of our times may be that too many couples—both Christian and non-Christian—are under the illusion that the best strategy for good marital sex is to seek a better marriage partner. Here Richard Hays is surely right that "those who have made promises before God should trust in God for grace sufficient to keep those promises, and they should expect the community of faith to help them keep faith, by supporting them and holding them accountable."[17] And David Matzko McCarthy is also right in maintaining that good sex should not be the only significant good sustaining love within marriage. Shared personal, spiritual, economic and civic goals—not least of which the nurturing of children—are also bonds that hold good marriages together. The romantic lens contributes to sexual insight, but only when put in its proper place as subordinate to the covenantal lens.

Contemporary essayist, novelist and poet Wendell Berry gives a moving description of marriage. Marriage, according to Berry,

> joins two living souls as closely as, in this world, they can be joined. This joining of two who know, love, and trust one another brings them in the same breath into the freedom of sexual consent and into the fullest earthly realization of the image of God. From their joining, other living souls come into being, and with them great responsibilities that are unending, fearful, and joyful. The marriage of two lovers joins them to one another, to forebears, to descendants, to the community, to Heaven and earth.[18]

Berry's mention of descendants points to the procreative view of sexuality and raises questions that have been debated between Protestants and Catholics. Would a voluntarily childless marriage be impoverished or impermissible? Can Christian couples use artificial contraception, or is contraceptive sex deficient—spiritually, morally or maritally? These questions are central to the debate about whether the covenantal lens should or should not be subordinate to the procreative lens.

As seen through the procreative lens, the goodness of sexual intercourse lies in its being life-transmitting. In order to preserve the goodness of sexuality, intercourse can appropriately take place only within conditions that allow for the nurturing and welfare of any resulting life. Children are vastly better off when cared for by both a mother and a father over the course of their whole lives. Thus, sexual intercourse is only appropriate to its nature when it takes place within a marriage—a lifelong commitment to one's spouse, the potential mother or father of resulting children. On this matter, the covenantal and procreative views agree. But those who see the procreative lens as central go beyond this, emphasizing that God intends our sexual organs to be used only "with good-hearted wisdom about the getting of children."[19] Uses of sexuality that are intentionally and intrinsically "unapt for generation" are thus perverse and morally impermissible. Rendering intercourse into a non-life-transmitting act perverts its very nature. On this procreative view contraceptive intercourse is not "a marriage act at all, whether or not we're married."[20]

Defenders of the centrality of the procreative lens have been breathtakingly courageous in their consistency. One such defender states that

> contraceptive intercourse within marriage is a graver offense against chastity than is straightforward fornication or adultery. For it is not even a proper act of intercourse, and *therefore* is not a true marriage act. To marry is not to enter into a pact of mutual complicity in no matter what sexual activity upon one another's bodies. (Why on earth should a ceremony like that of a wedding be needed or relevant if that's what's in question?) [21]

Medieval theologian Thomas Aquinas, whose theological works are the *locus classicus* of the Catholic position on sexuality, had some even more startling things to say. A relatively recent book by Catholic theologian John S. Grabowski, which is sympathetic to Aquinas's view, states, "For St. Thomas, the worst forms of lust are those that violate the natural procreative purpose of sex: bestiality, homosexual sex, non-vaginal heterosexual sex, and masturbation. Less grave expressions of lust are those that violate our relations with others: rape, adultery, seduction, and fornication."[22]

Grabowski sees himself as in accord not only with Aquinas but with Pope John Paul II, who asserted that sexual intercourse is "language of the body." According to John Paul II, intercourse is a "falsification of the inner truth of conjugal love" if it seeks to suppress the fertility of sexual union through any other means than periodic abstinence. "This is because fertility is not merely viewed as a biological aspect of the person that can be altered at his or her discretion, but like sexuality itself it is an existential reality (i.e., rooted in the order of existence) and pertains to the person as a whole."[23]

Catholics are aware that their views are not shared by the majority of modern Americans. For traditional Catholics the diagnosis for this is that our "contraceptive culture" has blinded people to the profound seriousness of sex, turning sexual interactions into shallow exchanges of bodily sensations and (in some cases) bodily fluids.

Those who take the covenantal lens to be central surely will also agree that being able to make a "bodily gift of oneself in love" within a committed relationship contributes to human flourishing.[24] Human beings are more likely to flourish if their sexual desires are not excessive or uncontrollable. There are indeed perverted sexual desires—desires that it would be dehumanizing to act on (necrophilia and pedophilia would be uncontroversial examples). Because of this, chastity is an important human virtue. Chastity, which we will discuss in more detail in chapter three, is the virtue that helps us focus our sexual energies on committed relationships and helps us treat our spouse as more than a means to sexual satisfaction. But through the covenantal lens, it does not follow from this that every use of contraception is perverse or unloving or unchaste.

In allowing for the use of contraception in marriage, those who take the covenantal lens as central are emphasizing and drawing out implications of themes that the procreative view also acknowledges. The procreative lens acknowledges that wholesome sex is life-uniting and that sexual relations that lack present delight hamper the bond between the couple. Fear of unwanted or untimely pregnancy within a committed marriage can reasonably be seen as hampering the life-uniting aspects of sex. Hoped-for children can still be acknowledged as central to marriage while using contraception as a way of planning the timing and spacing of the births of those children. This might contribute both to the flourishing of the husband and wife and to the flourishing of the children that result from their loving sexual relations. Here, because I take the procreative lens to be subordinate to the covenantal lens, I maintain that such uses of contraception do not violate the virtue of chastity.

Perhaps none of the other sexual lenses is transformed as much by being subordinated to the covenantal view than the power lens. Covenantal sexuality is tutored by the teaching that husbands are to love their wives as Christ loved the church and gave himself for it (Ephesians 5:25). Assertions of power and domination are to give way to mutual submission and concern within Christian marriage—in the bedroom no less than in other areas.

Yet Christians should not dismiss the power lens as irrelevant, for we need it to keep us on guard against our capacity for self-deception. Too often, Christian self-help books talk the language of covenant but are really recommending seeing sexuality as power. A memorable instance of this is Marabel Morgan's *The Total Woman*. This book was the bestselling nonfiction book of 1974. Its advice about how wives could "submit" to their husbands while getting their own way was wildly popular. The book's most famous recommendation was for a wife to wrap her naked body in plastic wrap and meet her husband at the front door. Though more recent books may not be so obvious in their recommendations of exploiting the power of our sexuality, the power lens can remind us to be critically reflective before we appropriate the advice of writers—even bestselling authors.

Sexuality can all too easily be deployed as a tool for manipulation, within marriage no less than outside it. I have more to say about this in chapter four on flirtation and seduction.

When Christians think, talk and live as if the covenantal lens is the only lens they use in viewing sexuality, they are prone to self-deception and distortion. Like everyone else, Christians are acculturated. How sexuality is viewed by Christians *will be* influenced by other sexual lenses within their surrounding culture. So it is important to be aware of how romantic, expressive, procreative, plain sex and power lenses are interacting with the covenantal lens that we are committed to using by our faith. When the covenantal lens is combined with others, yet is dominant and central to how those other lenses are deployed, we can show what well-ordered sexuality should look like. Sexuality's power to manipulate and objectify should be surrendered to its power to gratify and celebrate one's spouse's embodiment. Romantic attachment and sexual pleasure's expressive and procreative capacities should nurture and sustain marriages and stable families. When we live out our sexuality with the covenantal view ordering and perfecting the procreative, romantic, expressive, power and plain-sex views of sexuality, we can glorify God with our bodies.

3

VIRGINITY AND CHASTITY

Natalie Dylan was twenty-two years old in 2009 when she gained considerable attention for a brief time. She claimed that she had been offered $3.8 million dollars for her virginity through an Internet auction. Why would someone try to "sell her virginity"? Why would someone buy it?

Virginity, of course, cannot literally be bought and sold—no one can transfer their virginity to someone else. What Ms. Dylan was attempting to sell was sex, but supposedly a special kind of sex—intercourse with a person who had never had intercourse before. One commentator guessed that such an opportunity with an attractive woman might be viewed as a "trophy." What kind of trophy is being someone's "first time"?

The idea of sexual trophies is embedded in the power view of sexuality. Intellectual historian Betty Becker-Theye points out an interesting link between one's status as a seducer and the inexperience of one's "conquest." She says that "the myth of the seducer always touches upon the myth of the virgin." In the traditional stereotype, the seducer gains prestige by awakening a woman from a state of innocence. Virgins are highly valued targets for seduction because of their inaccessibility, and because the man who is a woman's "first time" goes where no other man has yet been allowed to go. Virgins are a challenge and a prize.[1]

As Becker-Theye makes clear, the concept of seduction has been traditionally intertwined with a sexual double standard that assumes that women, in contrast to men, should value their virginity. Seduction of a female virgin is supposed to be an achievement because it is a hard-won conquest. The successful seducer has shown himself to be more attractive, more charming and more clever than other men who have not been able to possess the particular target of conquest. We will examine the relationship between sex-as-power and seduction in chapter four. Notice, though, that the struggle between the seducer and the virgin he seeks to seduce pits the power view of sexuality against the procreative and covenantal views. For it is within the procreative and covenantal views that virginity has value and significance.

Selling sex for money is a practice embedded in a confluence of the power view and the plain sex view (a dynamic that we will be exploring in chapter seven). But again, in this particular instance, the views through various lenses seem at war with one another. The only status-conferring element for the buyer in an Internet auction seems to stem from an ability to afford a startlingly high payment. But why pay at all? How can someone's virginity still be a trophy if she or he is willing to sell it?

Whatever Natalie Dylan's and her purported customer's motives were beyond achieving brief notoriety, this incident shows how convoluted sexual dynamics have become in our culture. At one level Dylan's auction shows that virginity is still valued, but this valuing seems twisted.

Virginity has, in some places and times, been seen as priceless—a sacred condition. Catholics have seen virginity as such an important aspect of holiness that they have taught that Mary the mother of Jesus remained a perpetual virgin. In the Catholic tradition, virgin martyrs were identified as particularly worthy of admiration. These were women, usually young, who were willing to die in order to preserve their sexual purity. But in our culture virginity has become a kind of joke, a gag that underlies movies like *The 40-Year-Old Virgin,* a box-office success.

Is Virginity Valuable?

Laura M. Carpenter explored the varied meanings given to virginity in twenty-first-century America. Her book *Virginity Lost: An Intimate Portrait of First Sexual Experiences* explains four different ways that her study's subjects thought about their "virginity loss."[2] Some people conceived of virginity as a gift to be preserved until it can be given to someone special. Such people are viewing virginity through a romantic lens, or possibly through a covenantal or procreative lens.[3] Another group saw virginity as a stigma to be hidden until one can be rid of it. This is one way that virginity looks through the power lens. A third group saw the loss of one's virginity as a passage in a process of sexual maturation. This is how the expressive and plain sex views see the transition from being virginal to having sexual intercourse for the first time. A fourth group saw virginity as an aspect of worship of God. These people are clearly using either a covenantal or procreative lens.

Carpenter herself favors the loss-of-virginity-as-a-step-in-a-process view. Her research found that first sexual experiences were often disappointing, both physically and emotionally, especially for females. Those who saw virginity loss as a passage in a process were "better equipped than members of other interpretive groups for dealing constructively with the awkward and unpleasant aspects of an often-imperfect experience." Carpenter continues, "In a sense, it was virtually impossible for people who drew on the passage metaphor *not* to achieve what they saw as the chief goal of virginity loss—learning something—no matter what went 'wrong' in the process."[4] The passage-in-a-process view, seeing sex through the plain sex or the expressive lens, focuses on sex as a skill. Skills take practice. Practice may not make perfect, but it is bound to result in improvement eventually. Yet Carpenter's recommendation to view one's "first time" as a step in a process amounts to keeping expectations so low that you cannot possibly be disappointed.

Carpenter finds various downsides to the other three ways of viewing virginity loss. Those who see their partner's virginity as a "trophy" or their own virginity as a "stigma" see sex through the power lens. They assume that "taking" someone's virginity confers prestige and that lacking sexual experience is disempowering. Carpenter found that those who saw virginity as a stigma had the lowest rates of contraception and safe sex. They were so concerned to hide their sexual inexperience that they were prone to deception, risky behavior and performance anxiety. She goes on to note, "The partners of the stigmatized may also fare poorly, to the extent that they are treated as a means to achieving the end of virginity loss."[5]

Carpenter's concern for those she calls "gifters" (who see sex through procreative, covenantal or romantic lenses) is that too often they are devastated when they end up "giving themselves" to partners who do not treat their gift as precious, or partners who do not reciprocate their emotional investment in the relationship. She thinks this risk of severe disappointment outweighs certain benefits that gifters may have. Her study found that gifters were more likely to practice birth control and safe sex, because their first intercourse occurred in an established relationship that facilitated communication and planning.[6]

Only two subjects in Carpenter's study used the act-of-worship construal of virginity. These people are clearly using either a procreative or covenantal lens. From those subjects' experience Carpenter concludes that "people whose religious beliefs encourage them to treat premarital virginity as an expression of faith do reap spiritual benefits from doing so."[7] If they successfully live out their commitment to remain virgins until marriage, they are also well protected against unintended pregnancy and sexually transmitted infections. Carpenter's concerns about this metaphor arise from other studies showing that many who pledge themselves to premarital chastity do not keep their pledge; moreover, they are less likely to practice safe sex during their first sexual intercourse than those using the virginity-loss-as-a-passage-in-a-process metaphor.

Carpenter's evaluations of the four paradigms she considers are based mainly on pragmatic concerns. But one can debate the symbolic import of virginity. In an interesting meditation on the virgin martyrs in her book *Cloister Walk,* author Kathleen Norris suggests that instead of seeing virgins as incomplete and lacking in experience, we should see a virgin as someone who refuses to be defined by others.[8] Many of the virgin martyrs had "an adamantine sense of self."[9] Such virgins are their own persons and refuse to give themselves away. Feminist writer Naomi Wolf shares Norris's concerns that contemporary young women confer too much power on males. Wolf thinks that both anxiety about the loss of virginity and buying into stereotypes of virgins as frigid cede the power of defining women to males. Society at large, she fears, tells girls:

> what boys do with them is more significant to their maturing than what they themselves choose to do. Instead we should be telling girls what they already know but rarely see affirmed: that the lives they lead inside their own self-contained bodies, the skills they attain through their own concentration and rigor, the unique phase in their lives during which they may explore boys and eroticism at their own pace—these are magical.[10]

What *should* virginity mean? This seems another way of asking what lenses give us the clearest view of what sex means and why sex matters.

THE VIRTUE OF CHASTITY

But perhaps "What should virginity mean?" is not, for most of us, the most helpful question to ask. Author Lauren Winner takes a covenantal view of sexuality, yet she is concerned about the way virginity is elevated within evangelical Christian circles. She says, "To organize one's Christian sexual ethic around virginity is to turn sexual purity and sexual sin into a light switch you can flip— one day you're sexually righteous, and the next day, after illicit loss of your virginity, you're a sinner."[11]

"What is chastity?" is a more illuminating question to explore. Chastity is sometimes misconstrued as a mere synonym for virginity. But unlike virginity, which is a bodily state, chastity is a virtue. Virginity is a state that one can lose or give away. Apart from casuistic debates about whether oral sex or mutual masturbation are or are not "sex," virginity is an all-or-nothing matter. Either you are a virgin or you are not. In unusual cases it is a lifelong calling. Sadly, in our culture some people who are unwilling virgins may see this as a lifelong stigma. For most human beings, virginity is a temporary state.

But chastity, as a virtue, is a very different matter. To see this we need to understand a few important aspects of virtue in general. Virtues are habits or settled dispositions to behave in ways that contribute to well-lived lives. Courage is a virtue, as are generosity, determination, kindness and gratitude. Virtues are marked by a feeling of naturalness and a sense of enjoyment when they are exercised. Brave people face danger with comparative ease; generous people delight in making the perfect gift. Being virtuous also comes in degrees. I'm not as cowardly as some, but many people are more courageous than I am. Virtue is something that one can approximate.

Virtue-oriented ethical theories are the earliest systematic accounts of ethics. These theories focused on traits of character, sorting them into those that contribute to human flourishing and those that detract from flourishing. Virtue ethics played a central role in the classical Greek philosophical tradition. The main ethical question for these Greeks was not "What should I do in this particular circumstance?" but "What sort of person should I be or become?" As we discussed in the introduction, the idea is that *right actions* are a natural outgrowth of *being the best sort of person*. Valuable character traits like honesty, courage, fair-mindedness, generosity, self-discipline and even-temperedness are to be cultivated; damaging character traits like cruelty, laziness, dishonesty and cowardice are to be avoided.

Aristotle was among the most influential early writers on virtue. His famous "doctrine of the mean" was an important guide to moral virtue.[12] Applying the Greek adage "everything in moderation" to human character, Aristotle thought that virtues were, in part, the "just right" amount of a disposition, while the two related vices on either side of a virtue were "too much" and "too little" of the quality in question. We can miss the mark in the case of courage, for example, by being either cowardly or foolhardy. We can miss the mark in the case of generosity by being either miserly or foolishly extravagant. Contemporary virtue-oriented ethical theories do not assume the doctrine of the mean applies to every virtue; they treat it at most as a rule of thumb. This is because some virtues don't seem to fit the pattern. Virtues like patience and justice, for example, do not seem to be associated with a vice of "too much." Thomas Aquinas created a synthesis of Aristotle's virtue ethics and Christian ethics, by showing how the virtues of faith, hope and love can transform such natural virtues as courage and justice. Virtue-oriented approaches have also found favor among Protestants; philosopher Robert C. Roberts is prominent among contemporary Protestant virtue ethicists. All virtue-oriented views attempt to discern the difference between character traits that contribute to living a fully human life and those that do not. They also share a common view about character formation—people become virtuous or come to lack virtue by acting repeatedly in the same way. Virtues and vices are habits, and as habits become deeply ingrained through repetition and reinforcement, they become entrenched and hard to change.[13]

Virtue-oriented ethics focuses on character. The two main alternatives to virtue-oriented approaches focus instead on actions. Duty-oriented ethical views formulate rules about how to act derived from obligations, while consequence-oriented views hold that actions are required that optimize the positive outcomes of choices. We will have considerably more to say about duty-oriented and consequence-oriented approaches to ethics in chapters six and seven, because these approaches are widely deployed by ethicists in discussions of casual sex, sexual assault, pornography and prostitution.

In considering the virtue of chastity, it is important to remember something that Aristotle taught us long ago—that states of character range along a continuum. There is a difference between being virtuous and being well-behaved. A person may be well-behaved but have to struggle to do the right thing. Such a person, Aristotle points out, is not virtuous, but "continent"—able to successfully resist when he or she is tempted to misbehave. In my own case, I often have to wrestle with my ingrained stinginess in order to do the generous thing. Those who struggle to keep their behavior on target may be striving to rehabituate themselves toward virtue, but they are not yet virtuous. So struggle can be a sign of health—the growing pains of character. Someday, generosity may come more naturally to me. Then I will have moved from continence to virtue in this area.

If we think of virtue as at the top of the spectrum of states of character, then continence is the next best thing. Third best, after continence, is incontinence. Like the continent, the incontinent struggle to do the right thing; unlike the continent, the inconti-

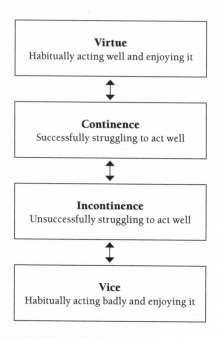

Figure 3

nent fail. But although struggle is painful and failure is even more painful, even unsuccessful struggle can be a sign of relative health. This is because at the bottom of the scale of states of character is vice—the settled disposition to behave badly and enjoy it. A person with a settled disposition to behave badly doesn't struggle. Thoroughly stingy people pride themselves on their "thrift," blissfully unaware that they fail to honor friendships by giving cheap, tacky gifts or token contributions to charity—or not giving anything at all. Their behavior comes so naturally to them that they hardly notice there might be other ways of behaving.

I like Lauren Winner's emphasis on chastity in her book *Real Sex: The Naked Truth about Chastity*. Her characterization of chastity is "doing sex in the Body of Christ—doing sex in a way that befits the Body of Christ, and that keeps you grounded, and bounded, in the community."[14] This characterization is helpful, but often when Winner discusses chastity she lapses into talking about it as a rule rather than a virtue. Chastity, she says, means "abstinence if you're not married, and fidelity if you are."[15] Winner also calls chastity a discipline, but the discipline seems to be a matter of following this rule. Thus Winner waffles between taking a virtue-oriented approach to chastity and taking a duty-oriented approach.

Catholic moral theology actually yields a more helpful definition of the virtue of chastity, emphasizing that chastity is the successful integration of sexuality within a person that results in inner unity between bodily and spiritual being.[16] Those who are chaste are fully at peace with their bodies and their sexuality. Chastity is not best seen as the ability to keep oneself from violating the sexual "rules"; rather, it is "a dynamic principle enabling

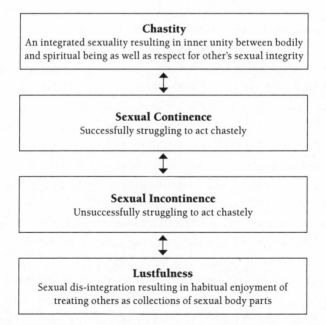

Chastity
An integrated sexuality resulting in inner unity between bodily and spiritual being as well as respect for other's sexual integrity

Sexual Continence
Successfully struggling to act chastely

Sexual Incontinence
Unsuccessfully struggling to act chastely

Lustfulness
Sexual dis-integration resulting in habitual enjoyment of treating others as collections of sexual body parts

Figure 4

one to use one's sexual powers intelligently in the pursuit of human flourishing and happiness."[17]

If chastity is a virtue, it is an aspect of character that a person can aspire to, achieve, stray from, regain. Notice that when the virtue at the top of this spectrum is chastity, there are three different ways of being unchaste—continence, incontinence and the vice of lustfulness.

The lustful take their behavior as a matter of course. Consider this comment by an adolescent male about what he would do if someone he were interested in said no to having sexual intercourse: "What I would do is carry on for a little bit by saying 'come on, come on, are you sure?' and I would tease them and s— like that . . . and after about a half an hour or so, and they still say no, I would let up. I would say 'don't worry, give me a blow job or a hand job instead.'"[18] This young man's perceptions of sexuality are so colored by the plain sex and power lenses that he has no awareness of his own exploitive and manipulative strategies.

Lustfulness seems like fun to the lustful, but seen through the covenantal, procreative or romantic lens, it falls short of human flourishing. It dehumanizes others and oneself. "Desire informed by chastity is desire for the other as a person—it views the sexual qualities of the person in the light of his or her personal dignity. Lust abstracts the person's sexual traits and focuses on them apart from their dignity. It thus reduces the person so regarded to an object of use and enjoyment rather than viewing that person as worthy of respect and love."[19] Chastity, as a virtue, is not just the ability to "do without sex" for weeks or months. Among other things, it keeps our sexual desires from making us view others as collections of sexually arousing body parts.

Those who are continent with regard to their sexuality successfully struggle against lust—realigning their attention when they find themselves objectifying others and making every effort to abide by the "abstinence in singleness and fidelity in marriage" rule. How much of a struggle this is for a given person may vary depending on circumstances. One likely predictor of whether one will be sexually continent or sexually incontinent is how well one knows oneself. Self-knowledge can help people manage their environment and their desires so that struggle need not be heroic in order to succeed. Whether the apostle Paul was talking about sexual incontinence or some other besetting lapse of virtue in Romans 7 is unknown, but his description of the anguish of incontinence is moving: "For I do not do the good I want, but the evil I do not want is what I do. . . . Wretched man that I am! Who will rescue me from this body of death?" (Romans 7:19, 24).

Neither continence nor incontinence is anywhere near as fun as virtue. Once a virtue has become second nature, it gives a settled sense of joy. When you meet people who have a truly integrated sexuality, a psychological and physical unity, they seem happily and robustly embodied. They aren't all fidgety, restless, self-conscious, driven, lustful. They are content, yet aware and appreciative of their own body and those of others. They are erotic without "making moves" or ogling, leering or vamping. And here's the thing: some of these people are happily married and some of these people are happily single.

And here's another thing: it is an extraordinarily rare human being who has never been unchaste.

I have met people who are chaste, who are at home in their bodies and are fully integrated sexual beings. I doubt very much that they were always such. Adolescence is turbulent. Extended adolescence, in the sense of sexual restlessness and reticence to make lasting commitments, is becoming a cultural commonplace. Without social support, virtues like chastity are difficult to cultivate. For many, sexual integrity may seem like a distant goal. Within the church this puts them in good company. After all, Augustine is famous for praying, "Grant me chastity and continence, but not yet."[20]

Societies that care about sexual boundaries have recognized that chastity is rare. Some of these societies seem extraordinarily restrictive to us, and almost all of them have made women bear a disproportionate share of the burden of that restrictiveness. The burqa and the Medieval "chastity belt" (worn by the lady while her knight was away in battle) are examples of social "solutions" to the perception that continence is fragile and chastity is rare. Female circumcision appears to many in the West to be a brutal attempt to inscribe chastity onto the female body. There are more humane and more gender-neutral solutions: the age-old and transcultural custom of the chaperone is one.

Unlike these extreme examples of restrictive societies, the wider culture we presently inhabit gives no social support to developing chastity or exercising sexual continence. Chastity is rarer than continence and incontinence, yet it is an extraordinarily useful virtue, no matter what one's life circumstances are. One does not need to be a Catholic or a proponent of the procreative view to appreciate the aptness of Pope John Paul II's characterization of chastity as self-mastery that makes the gift of oneself in love possible.[21]

Catholics naturally discuss the chastity needed by celibates considerably more than Protestants do. Celibate chastity is the ability to happily dedicate all of one's life, including one's sexuality, to the service of God in a way that permanently foregoes marriage. But chastity has a far wider application than celibacy. Both the median age of first marriage and life expectancy are rising in the United States. We are now reaching the point in our culture where most people who live into old age will spend most of their lives unmarried. Chastity allows unmarried or widowed people not only to refrain from inappropriate sexual expression but to direct their erotic energies in ways that contribute to their own flourishing and that of other people. Chastity also then allows them to be capable of making a total bodily gift of self to another when (and if) they eventually marry or remarry.

And chastity is not just for the single. Chastity allows married people to give the gift of their genital sexual expression to one other person as a "bodily gift of self." It allows them to be comfortably centered emotionally and erotically within their marriage. Chastity helps married couples refrain from treating one another as just convenient means to satisfying their appetites. And chastity helps healthy spouses deal with their sexual appetites when their spouses are sexually unavailable because of health challenges.

When Lauren Winner says, "Chastity is tough,"[22] she is really talking about sexual continence. Both continence and advancing from continence to chastity *are* tough. In contrast, chastity is comfortable—a blessing really. It's also relatively rare, at least in its unalloyed form. Its rarity and blessedness make it a fitting object for a quest. The quest for chastity is the quest for sexual integrity.

PART THREE

Complications—
Where Clarity Is a Challenge

FLIRTATION AND SEDUCTION

A skilled flirt is often a joy to watch. Skilled flirts exude confident embodiment and express appreciation for the embodied presence of others. Innocent flirtation can be energizing, both for the one doing the flirting and the person being flirted with.

Skilled flirts can also be destructively manipulative. The subtle and not-so-subtle ways we convey that we find others physically attractive fall along a spectrum, with innocent flirtation at one end and exploitive seduction at the other. *Seduce* has its root in the Latin *seducere,* to lead away or separate. To seduce is to lead someone away from his or her own principles or best judgment.[1] Yet how many people reflect much about when flirtation is a social good and when it grades off toward seduction and becomes a source of harm?

Hundreds of movies, music videos, commercials, novels, magazines, blogs and self-help books provide role models and guidance on how to invite sexual interest from others. We may not be looking for advice in this area. Nonetheless, we are being shaped, unreflectively, by these stories and models. We are being shaped by them whether or not we want to be and whether or not they are based on wisdom or folly. Sexuality is not just about intercourse

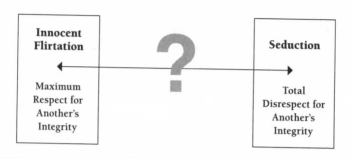

Innocent Flirtation	?	Seduction
Maximum Respect for Another's Integrity		Total Disrespect for Another's Integrity

Figure 5

or even just about intercourse and foreplay. We take our sexuality with us wherever we go. If whether and when to engage in sexual intercourse is the sole focus of our quest for sexual insight, we will be blind to vast regions of our sexuality in our day-to-day lives. Consider three stories I have heard firsthand.

Sam was seventeen and excited to be making good money waiting tables at a family-style restaurant. After working there about a month, he'd become a sort of mascot among the experienced wait staff, almost all females several years older than him. They took him under their wing and encouraged him when he made beginner mistakes. They got a good laugh over Sam's accidentally spilling ice water down a customer's back and then charming the customer enough with his apology to secure a generous tip. Then a new waitress, Kristen, was hired. Kristen started showing him a different kind of attention. She leaned in close when talking; touching him on his arm or chest. She gave him admiring compliments about his build. She caressed his back when they passed on the way back and forth from the kitchen. Sam was simultaneously flattered and uncomfortable. Another waitress, Wanda, took Sam aside one day and warned him. Kristen had offered a wager to several coworkers. She had bet that she could get Sam in bed with her by the end of her first week at the restaurant. Sam was angry, but mainly he found Kristen's game-playing pathetic.

Ann was chatting with a group of friends at a party when three of her graduate-school classmates joined the circle. These guys had arrived together and reported that they had been talking on the way to the party about how much they each admired Ann. Two of them engaged her in lighthearted banter about how they'd have wanted to date her and were a bit sad that she was already married. Ted, the third man, was mainly quiet while his friends talked, but nodded his agreement that, as one of the other guys put it, "they were all a little bit in love with her." As the party unfolded and Ted had a few drinks, he asked Ann to dance. She agreed but started getting uncomfortable as he returned to the subject of how attracted he was to her. Could they have lunch sometime soon? She turned down this invitation and, after the dance ended, headed to the far side of the room and joined another conversation group. Ted followed her, asking for another dance. She thanked him but said she'd rather not. As the night wore on, he became more persistent as he became more intoxicated. When she stopped being willing to talk to him, he talked loudly with others about how cruel life was when the woman he "loved" wouldn't even agree to lunch. Ann left the party as soon as she could and wondered how she'd handle crossing paths with Ted in the future.

Lori and Ben had been friends for quite some time. They worked together and had socialized as family units. They had more interests in common than their spouses did, but they had children of similar ages and often went on outings where the adults could talk while the children played together. Looking back, they disagreed about who had started the pattern of increasingly personal disclosures. Their one-on-one conversations increased in length and frequency. Lori realized that somehow they'd crossed the line when Ben started writing poems dedicated to her. They started having many convoluted conversations about how to reassert proper boundaries. When these failed, Ben and Lori decided that their friendship had morphed into a threat to their marriages.

Their disagreement about who was at fault and what they should do corroded their friendship. There was no big drama—no affair. All their spouses ever knew was that somehow the families met less frequently, but Ben and Lori both regretted having traded a healthy friendship for a flirtation.

These stories illustrate the ambiguities surrounding flirtation. As one philosopher writing on the topic notes, flirtation eroticizes the parts of our lives that we cannot control. Flirtation turns "doubt—or ambiguity—into suspense."[2] One recent study on adolescent sexuality found that "ambiguity was a key feature of sexual communication."[3] Ambiguity can protect individuals from embarrassment and rejection. Ambiguity can guard them from presumption. As one of the research subjects asserted, "You're not going to come out with 'I'm not going to sleep with you tonight,' because that makes him think you thought you could."[4] People want to avoid coming right out and asking for sex. People also want to avoid flat-out rejection of sexual advances (especially if they are ambiguous). Hence our culture, over time, has developed the elaborate ritual of flirtation and response.

THE NATURE OF FLIRTATION

If I flirt with someone, I participate in forms of social behavior that are understood to send the message that I am attracted to him. I hold eye contact in a certain way; I lean into the usual margin separating people as they converse; I touch a hand or arm; I hold my body in "that certain way"—hard to describe but easily recognized. By behaving in this way, I also send the message that I'd welcome signs of being attractive to the person with whom I am flirting. I invite the other person to flirt back. The suspense is, "Will he (or she) or won't he (or she)?" By launching into this behavior, I go out on a limb, and the risk itself can be thrilling. If not reciprocated, and especially if explicitly rebuffed, my flirtation risks at least mild humiliation on my part. The more ambiguous my flirtatiousness is, the less risk there is of humiliation. No response? Well, I wasn't really interested anyway; I'm just outgoing and friendly by nature. And plausible deniability is not just self-protective but can give the person who is being flirted with a graceful out as well. By refusing to interpret flirtatious behavior as flirtation, the recipient who is not interested sends that message without having to say it in so many words. Both parties run risks but often both parties can save face.

Yet ambiguity carries its own risks. If my flirtation is too subtle, my message may not be received—the person I am attracted to may not perceive my attraction. More dangerously, ambiguity allows for miscommunication, self-deception and manipulation. The line between flirtation and treating someone as a sex object is not always obvious, nor is the line between flirtation and sexual harassment. Subjecting someone to sexual advances knowing that such interest is unwelcome treats them as a sex object. Even making known one's sexual thoughts can involuntarily make someone else a party to fantasies that they would find obscene.[5] Yet as Katie Roiphe observes, "To find wanted sexual attention, you have to give and receive a certain amount of unwanted sexual attention. Clearly, the truth is that if no one ever was allowed to risk offering unsolicited sexual attention, we would all be solitary creatures."[6] These dynamics fill the dating scene with anxiety.

One difference between sexual harassment and flirtation is that flirtation stops when someone flirting perceives that his or her sexual attentions are unwanted, but harassment continues. Another difference between flirtation and sexual harassment depends on *how* sexual interest is conveyed. Flirtation is subtle, playful, and when done well, artistic and charming. Some ways of conveying sexual interest are so crude, demeaning or intrusive that any reasonable person would know that they are inappropriate as a first interpersonal overture.

The ambiguity inherent in flirtation can be abused as well as used. "I didn't mean anything by it" may in some cases be a very lame excuse. In other cases it might be an acknowledgment of guilt. Innocent flirtation too easily morphs into game-playing under the protective cover of plausible deniability. In many instances, if you flirt you *should* "mean it" or at least know that what you intend to convey is appropriate in the context and hasn't been misunderstood.

FLIRTATION AND THE SIX LENSES

Here, as elsewhere, paying attention to our sexual lenses can help us see more clearly. Let me briefly sketch out these various perspectives before looking more closely at flirtation and seduction themselves.

The romantic lens will look favorably on flirtation among unattached adults as a way of looking for Mr. or Ms. Right. Flirtation is a part of showing interest and paying compliments; it's a natural part of dating. Once one has found one's true love, flirtation within one's romance may keep the spark alive. But the romantic will frown upon showing sexual interest in others outside one's primary relationship. Flirting outside a committed relationship looks like emotional infidelity. Seduction, as a concerted plan to overcome the will of someone in whom you are romantically interested, will be seen as ambiguous. In most instances it will look like manipulation—perhaps even like stalking or assault. Oddly, though, seduction is a prominent motif in romance novels. For romantics, perhaps seduction is acceptable only in those fairy-tale-like situations where the seduced and the seducer were destined to be "soul mates" all along.

The expressive lens will see flirtation as a healthy and playful manifestation of sexuality. What could be more natural than people finding others attractive and wanting to show appreciation and invite mutual interest? Expressivists, being less committed to monogamy than romantics, will view flirtation as acceptable whether or not one limits it to finding a primary sexual partner.

The plain sex view will see expressing sexual interest, and being skillful at generating the sexual interest of others, as tools for maximizing sexual satisfaction. Yet because the plain sex view generally respects the rights of others to decline sexual advances, rebuffs will be taken with good grace. The plain sex flirt will move on to other hunting grounds if an overture fails to elicit interest.

The power lens is likely to see flirtation, and perhaps even seduction, as reasonable strategies for sexual self-assertion, even if the goal is a one-night stand. The suspense that heightens the drama as seen by the romantic view ("Are you the one?" "Will we find true love?") is seen by the power view as the thrill of the chase—which is really about power or self-aggrandizement, not romance. The power flirt may be expressing appreciation for the embodied presence of another, but at bottom the goal is always to assert one's own attractiveness and sexual power. And the power lens will see seduction as a natural strategy for finding sexual partners. After all, "all's fair in love and war."

The procreative and covenant lenses, as they are embedded in the Christian tradition, see flirtation as itself problematic if the flirt's intent is to awaken the sexual or romantic interest of another where there is no serious possibility of long-term commitment. Flirtation, even as a part of dating behavior among the unmarried, can entice lust. Flirtation can raise expectations that the flirt has no intention of acting upon. Yet flirtation as a sincere exploration of possibilities that might lead to commitments may be allowed. In contrast to the plain sex view, the procreative and covenantal lens will see flirtation, when used as recreation with no serious intent, as problematic.[7]

Seduction, with its lack of respect for the integrity of another, would clearly be impermissible within the covenantal view. Christians know that we all "see through a glass, darkly" (1 Corinthians 13:12 KJV) and that it is all too easy to lose track of one's true self. Our central good is the fulfillment, or at least the approximation, of God's intentions for us. Within the Christian story, loving knowledge involves and makes possible the work of attention necessary for insight into God's intentions for one's loved ones and neighbors. Within the Christian story, resistance to the seducer is not just standing up for oneself; resistance to being co-opted into someone else's self-deception and distortion is the most loving response one can make to someone who has lost his or her way. God woos us without disrespecting our will; in our pursuit of godliness and sexual integrity we should emulate God's respectful yet ever-seeking love.

THE DYNAMICS OF FLIRTATION

Flirtation has its natural home in the romantic and expressive views of sexuality. To understand flirtation better it will be helpful to look at a detailed analysis of its dynamics. Philosopher Thomas Nagel wrote an essay in the 1970s on the nature of sexual desire. Nagel wanted to emphasize that normal sexual desire is something more than a desire to interact with someone else's body, but has to do with how we perceive others and how we value being perceived. Nagel's point was that sexual desire makes you vividly aware of your own body—both your body's embodied responses to desire but also its ability to awaken the desire of another, and that these awarenesses are mutually reinforcing and mutually escalating. Sexual desire, says Nagel (in typically clunky philosophical prose), "involves the desire that one's partner be aroused by the recognition of one's desire that he or she be aroused."[8]

To illustrate his ideas about multilevel mutual arousal, Nagel asks his reader to imagine a man, Romeo, sitting in a cocktail lounge with many mirrors on the walls. These mirrors are at different angles; their reflections and refractions permit people sitting in the lounge to observe others without obviously staring directly at them. Romeo looks into one of the mirrors and spots Juliet's reflection. Something about her hair and the line of her neck begins to arouse his sexual desire.

Juliet, unbeknownst to Romeo, is observing Romeo in another mirror and, by happy coincidence, is also sexually attracted to him. "Romeo then begins to notice in Juliet the subtle signs of sexual arousal, heavy-lidded stare, dilating pupils, faint flush, etc."[9] As Romeo notices Juliet's arousal, this intensifies his own arousal. At this point, Nagel asserts that Romeo's "arousal is nevertheless still solitary," because Romeo does not know that Juliet's desire is aimed at *him*. But then Romeo calculates the sightlines of the mirrors and realizes that Juliet is not just aroused, but *desires him*. If she, in turn, has her arousal intensified by becoming aware that he is aroused by her, Romeo will have a heightened sense of his own sexuality and its effects. Nagel imagines that if they are each alone, they will turn toward one another, introduce themselves, and a romantic encounter will unfold.

Nagel's tale of Romeo and Juliet serves a particular purpose in his essay. His project was to define sexual perversion by contrasting it with normal sexuality. What is normal for humans, Nagel hypothesizes, is desire premised upon "some version of reciprocal interpersonal sexual awareness."[10] Sexual perversion arises when the development of this mutuality of awareness is blocked or distorted, as in fetishism (being aroused by inanimate objects) or bestiality (being aroused by nonhuman animals) or necrophilia (being aroused by corpses). Voyeurism, exhibitionism and pedophilia also short-circuit the normal dynamic of multilevel mutual arousal, albeit in more complex ways.

Philosopher Janice Moulton subsequently pointed out that Nagel is not really describing the structure of normal sexual desire. Sexual desire between couples in established and long-standing relationships, including marriages, won't always have the structure that Nagel describes. What Nagel is actually capturing in his vignette are the dynamics of sexual anticipation, flirtation and seduction.

Much of the drama of Nagel's tale of Romeo and Juliet comes from our sense that, at the outset, neither Romeo nor Juliet knows what will happen next. He sees her. He's attracted. But until he sees signs that she is attracted and that her attraction is attraction *to him,* he has no reason to believe that his evening will hold more than a solitary drink followed by a solitary dinner followed by going home alone.

Nagel's "multilevel mutual arousal" reveals the structure of flirtation. But Nagel's cocktail lounge of mirrors has the effect of reducing the risk that is normally present in flirtation to some degree. Much, if not all, of the risk in Nagel's vignette is felt by the reader: Will these two both plot the sightlines correctly; will they come to know that they are attrac*tive* to one another and not just attrac*ted* to one another? The mirrors, because they allow for unobserved observation, reduce the risk felt by Romeo and by Juliet to a minimum. Romeo and Juliet turn to direct interpersonal interaction only *after* discerning their mutual attraction.

For this reason, the vignette hovers between the structure of flirtation and the structure of voyeurism. In flirtation I care whether the person I find attractive perceives my attraction and becomes attracted to me in return. Flirtation risks rejection or failure to be understood. The voyeur's arousal does not depend on whether the person who arouses him or her is aroused by the voyeur him- or herself. The voyeur does not risk rejection; the voyeur is safe as long as the voyeur can observe without being observed. Voyeurism has its home in the power view, for its pleasures are rooted in self-protection at the expense of transgressing the personal space of another.

Nagel's tale of Romeo and Juliet seems like an outline for a mildly interesting modern urban fairytale because Romeo's and

Juliet's attraction ends up being mutual. But suppose that Romeo calculates the sightlines in the cocktail lounge and finds that Juliet's arousal is dependent on her observation of some third party. If Romeo is not disappointed by this, but instead more intensely titillated, getting a charge out of watching Juliet enact Nagel's scenario with some *other* person in the bar, Romeo turns into a much darker (or sadder) character. If Juliet comes to know that Romeo has been watching all this time and that he's been getting a charge out of unobserved observation of her, and if she has no interest in him, her likely responses will range from disdain to anger or fear. Flirting seems fun, harmless. Voyeurism and seduction have a different feel.

The Dynamics of Seduction

As with flirtation, it will be helpful to take a careful look at the dynamics of seduction. In doing so, I will carefully examine the play *Les Liaisons Dangereuses*,[11] adapted by Christopher Hampton from the eighteenth-century novel of the same name by Choderlos de Laclos. *Les Liaisons Dangereuses* is a play about seduction.[12]

Hampton's character the Vicomte de Valmont had a female friend, Marquise de Merteuil, with whom he shared a common hobby—seduction. For years they have compared notes on the conquests they have made. As the action of the play begins, they make a wager: Merteuil will have sex with Valmont if he succeeds in seducing Madame de Tourvel, who is a woman famous for her "strict morals, religious fervor and the happiness of her marriage."[13]

Valmont relishes the challenge of seducing someone who appears unseducible. This will be the supreme demonstration of his irresistibility. Early in the play he tells Merteuil, "I have no intention of breaking down [Madame de Tourvel's] prejudices. I want her to believe in God and virtue and the sanctity of marriage, and still not be able to stop herself. . . . I want the excitement of watching her betray everything that's most important to her."[14] Valmont relishes watching Madame de Tourvel being torn between her growing interest in him and her personal integrity.

Valmont sets out to systematically undermine Madame de Tourvel's defenses. He arranges to be a houseguest where Madame de Tourvel is staying and soon declares his love for her. When she asks him to leave her alone, he agrees to vacate the house, but begs her to accept his correspondence. Madame de Touvel is a devout Catholic, and when his letters become too passionate for her to find acceptable, Valmont connives to have her confessor insist that she allow Valmont an audience in order to beg her forgiveness for offending her. Again and again Valmont uses Madame de Touvel's sympathy for his plight as an unrequited lover as an opening to pursue his goal. He enjoys using her own virtues to snare her. As he tells his friend the Marquise: "Her eyes are closing. Every step she tries to take away from the inevitable conclusion brings her a little nearer to it."[15] He finally convinces de Tourvel that if she does not sleep with him, he will commit suicide. This brings about her tearful acquiescence; she sacrifices her integrity for his life and happiness. The Marquise, who has by now become jealous of what she suspects is a real attachment of Valmont to Madame de Tourvel, refuses to "pay off" on their wager. Instead she indicates that Valmont must break off his connection with Madame de Tourvel or risk looking ridiculous—conquered rather than a conqueror. He coldly breaks with de Tourvel; she commits suicide.

Hampton's dark play displays sexuality used in the service of raw power. For Vicomte de Valmont and Marquise de Merteuil sex is a competitive sport where the point is to see how many others one can enthrall without becoming enthralled. Valmont's cold-bloodedness, his relishing of the very features of the case that will render the situation most devastating for Madame de Tourvel, his calculated exploitation of her virtues to maneuver her to his goal, his holding her up to the scrutiny and ridicule of the Marquise—all make his behavior more odious than it would be otherwise.

Valmont's seduction of Madame de Tourvel involves features that are present in a broader spectrum of cases of seduction.

- There is mutual consent to all sexual activities at the time of participation.

- The pursuer seeks knowledge of the pursued in order to use that knowledge for purposes of obtaining consent to sexual activity.

- Deception, or at least calculated ambiguity, is used as a means to obtaining consent to sexual activity.

- The pursuer is indifferent to the welfare of the pursued, or at least takes the pursued's welfare only as an easily overridden priority.

- The pursuer's motives in the pursuit are personal pleasure and self-aggrandizement.

- The pursued person consents to sexual activities that he or she was (at least initially) adverse to engaging in or that are at odds with his or her principles or priorities.

- The pursued person would not consent to all the activities engaged in unless he or she were deceived or manipulated.

It is a common cultural assumption that seducers are male, though the female as seductress is also a common trope. Note that the features of seduction listed here involve no assumptions made about gender roles. A seducer could be male or female, as could the person pursued.

The presence of consent is essential to seduction, for consent is what distinguishes seduction from rape (see chapter six for an extensive discussion of the ethical importance of sexual consent). Consent is also part of what normally makes the situation enjoyable for the seducer. Getting to yes is intrinsic to the game; being able to get a yes where others would meet continued resistance is what makes the seduction an ego-enhancing experience for the seducer.

If seduction leads to consensual sex, then why is seduction problematic? Seducers show a negligent or callous disregard for the central good of those whom they pursue. The seducer sets out to procure consent to sexual activity without caring whether sex will compromise elements that are integral to the other's values and sense of self.

The seducer lives as if he or she is ignorant of the truth that each of our lives is lived with and among others who have their own stories to live out and tell. The seducer's purposes and plans fail to take into account the fact that others also have purposes and plans. The seducer's version of how things are does not take into account that others have differing versions of their story.

The seducer sets out to know someone with the intent of abusing the power that such intimate knowledge confers. The seducer uses his or her knowledge not for the purpose of aiding the other in discerning and pursuing his or her destiny, but to win compliance with the seducer's own agenda, whether or not that agenda is likely to conflict with how the other's life should unfold.

Philosopher Onora O'Neill points out that detailed, intimate knowledge of another's character and desires makes it all too easy to make someone "an offer he or she cannot refuse." Deception and coercion aren't necessary if you know someone well enough to understand how they can be maneuvered.[16] Seduction is wrong because exploiting such personal knowledge is a failure of respect and benevolence. Intimacy is used as a weapon or lever, rather than cherished as a gift. Respect and benevolence require giving due attention to the plans and projects people consciously pursue and acknowledge as their own. Consequently, we must refrain from setting out to win sexual consent without regard to its effect on another's central plans or values.

Innocent flirtation issues an invitation and leaves its acceptance up to the other person. Seduction sets out to circumvent the sexual autonomy of the other person. But there are many points and complications along the spectrum between these two poles. There are, for example, the stages of courtship when gradually increasing intimate knowledge of one's intended doesn't fit neatly into either the category of flirtation nor that of seduction, since the level of intimacy has passed flirtation yet the goal is not exploitation. And there is the invitation to sexual creativity that one spouse may give to another through gestures or other means. Such invitations may be deeply erotic and be issued from the same kind of intimate knowledge exploited by the seducer, yet undermining sexual integrity is neither their goal nor their result. There is also (to take an example that is both more problematic and less intimate) the exploitive flirt, who through body language, innuendo or sexualized dress, seeks to excite sexual interest solely with the intent of stoking his or her own ego. Though this may not lead to actual sexual contact, it still may do damage by undermining another's dignity or sexual continence.

Yet another example would be the paternalistic "seducer" who sets out to lure someone into an adventurous type of sexual expression in order to rid him or her of hang-ups that the seducer deems are best shed. If the seducer is genuinely interested in the good of the other, is it really wrong to circumvent the current values of the person being seduced? Such a seducer might think that he or she knows the other so intimately that his or her knowledge is deeper and more reliable than the other's self-knowledge. While in some cases this may be true, the risks for self-delusion here are serious. We are on morally shaky ground when we set out to be paternalistic in nonsexual contexts toward anyone but our own adolescent and preadolescent children (or others who are in our charge and who are below the age of reason). Paternalism is no less dangerous in areas of sexuality. In cases where we think we know more than our beloved does about what is sexually good for them, discussion is a morally safer, though less titillating, alternative than seductive stratagems.

As we saw earlier, the ambiguity inherent in flirtation can heighten the drama of social interaction; it can eroticize the accidents of our lives. Flirtation can let each of us explore a romantic possibility while protecting ourselves or someone else from severe embarrassment in cases where the interest turns out not to be mutual. Sexual insight can help us know when the line is crossed from the *use* of ambiguity to the *abuse* of ambiguity. The quest for sexual integrity will always encourage a focus on the best for all with whom we interact.

Seduction may look "romantic" to some, but it is really all about power. Coercion is all too common in sexual exchanges, and awareness of the power lens can help us see where it is operative. The hookup culture on many college campuses, which is an often toxic mix of the plain sex and power views of sexuality, has made the question of when seduction becomes rape a heated debate. Chapter six will give us an extensive opportunity to explore these matters. But before turning to that discussion, we will be examining a cluster of issues related to homosexuality in the next chapter.

HOMOSEXUALITY

I moved to the Bay Area," said Chris. Even though it was California, I didn't know how my coworkers would react. So I started slow. First I told them, 'I'm Jewish.' Once I saw that they were okay with that, I let them know I am gay."

Chris, a participant in a national academic administrators' workshop that I attended in 2010, shared this snippet of personal history in group discussion. The session was focused on "identities" in the workplace—race, ethnicity, gender, religion, social class—and how they affect working relationships. Chris recounted hesitancies about self-disclosure as illustrations of how complicated "identity" can be in the workplace.

Chris was talking about the felt necessity of being attuned to others' attitudes, about feeling initially unsafe around strangers. Disclosure was not and could not be a haphazard affair. Yet Chris is an employee of a large state university in one of the most liberal areas of the United States late in the first decade of the twenty-first century. How much more fear would surround disclosure within more conservative circles? Regardless of what lens Chris views sexuality through, Chris worried whether others would judge, disparage, shun and punish.

Perhaps you know firsthand what all this feels like. I don't—at least in this particular area. Most of us have aspects of ourselves we keep private. But for heterosexuals, the fact that we have sexual desires for the opposite sex is not one of those. Indeed, heterosexuals do not even consider whether to "disclose" our heterosexuality. We take for granted that others take our heterosexuality as a given.

UNIQUE ISSUES OF HOMOSEXUALITY

There are at least two layers of social and moral complexity for Christian homosexuals with which Christian heterosexuals do not have to deal.

One is the issue of how "out" to be about the orientation of their sexual attractions, whether or not they feel permitted to act on them through seeking a committed relationship or express those attractions through flirtation. Celibate or not, will they trust others with the knowledge of their orientation? If so, whom will they trust?

The other issue is whether there are any permissible options for homosexuals other than celibacy if they seek to be faithful Christians. Whereas the first issue is about social acceptance, the second issue is about whether the virtue of chastity will need to be lived out very differently for Christians who are homosexual than for Christians who are heterosexual.

The two Christian lenses share the view that sexual intercourse belongs within marriage. If there is theological space for gay marriage or for sanctified lifelong homosexual commitments, then sexual integrity for homosexuals will look very similar to sexual integrity for heterosexuals. If there is such a theological space, chapters two through four of this book will be applicable to homosexuals and heterosexuals alike without caveat. If there is no such space, then for all Christian homosexuals chastity will issue the challenge of seeking to become fully at home with their sexuality while practicing lifelong celibacy. This is a challenge faced by only a minority of Christian heterosexuals—those who, for a variety of reasons, never marry.

APPROACHING HOMOSEXUALITY WITH EMPATHY

Homosexuality, perhaps more than any other sexual issue, has historically been couched in terms of what "we" should say about "them." In order to guard against the judgmentalism I alluded to in the introduction, all of us, gay or straight, should cultivate both empathy and humility as elements of our process of discernment. If you are heterosexual, try to imagine how your life would be different if the world were turned upside down—if, like Chris, you often felt you had to conceal this pervasive aspect of who you are. How many small and large facts about yourself would you need to hide? Whatever you think about the issue of gay marriage, you should at least develop empathy for the extra challenges facing homosexuals. If you are homosexual, try to imagine how bewildered many heterosexuals are when they consider that sexual desires may be different for some people than everything they have known and have had culturally reinforced as both normal and normative.

None of us comes to the complex issues surrounding homosexuality without a frame shaped by our upbringing and personal experience. I was raised in a sheltered, conservative environment where I was well into adolescence before I'd even had the category "homosexual" introduced to me. It was many more years after that before I knew of someone who was homosexual. Even now, when I have friends who I know are homosexuals, I generally do not go through the world with the categories "homosexual" and "heterosexual" enough at the forefront of my mind for it to occur to me to wonder about people's orientation except under special circumstances—for example, when they bring it up. Looking back on my childhood, I realize that I must have hung around peer groups where either the other kids were just as clueless as I was or where the taboos were so strong that homosexuality was not mentioned. In a way, I think this makes me better off than my children, who by grade school in the early 1990s came home from playgrounds with distressing habits of using sexual slurs that I felt the need to stamp out. "Think about what yelling 'You f—' does to people; think what it does to you." (This is the kind of exhortation children of philosophers have to put up with.) My children grew out of these childish speech patterns long ago, but perhaps none of us is without baggage from the mix of insights, deficiencies and distortions that shaped our growing up.

No matter what our differing personal experiences have been, I suggest that there should be one minimal ethical and Christian common ground: No one should demean someone because of their sexual orientation. Should we go beyond that, as some recommend, to viewing homosexuality as on a par with left-handedness? Should we all be okay with homosexuality? Being "okay with homosexuality" embraces a wide range of approaches—from not being a "gay basher" (either literally or figuratively) to unreserved affirmation of homosexual activity, whether monogamous or not, as a legitimate alternative lifestyle. Where on the spectrum should we be if we seek to be faithful to Christian understandings of humanity and sexuality? Is God "okay" with homosexuality?

However we answer those questions, we need empathy as one tool for moral discernment about homosexuality, but our empathy needs to be expansive. Some of us need to work toward empathy for those who have same-sex desires and face all sorts of challenges because of that; others of us need to cultivate empathy with people whose convictions dictate stances with which we profoundly disagree. Personal narratives from divergent perspectives can help broaden the range of our empathy.

Over a cup of coffee after a recent worship service, a man we'd just met told my husband and me that he had been an Episcopa-

lian until a few years ago. He'd been raised an Episcopalian. But
though he had resonated with the liturgy and theology of that
denomination, he'd objected to the installation of an openly gay
bishop by American Episcopalians. He emphasized that he is "not
antigay." He just thought that ordaining gay bishops was "going
too far" and was saddened by the rift it had caused in the world-
wide Anglican community. Most Anglicans outside the U.S. continued to object to sexually active gay clergy. He missed the denomination that he still felt was in some sense his spiritual home,
but he felt as if American Episcopals had left *him* rather than the
other way around.

I have a friend whose convictions also motivated her to leave
her church, but for a contrasting reason. She left the congregation
where she was associate pastor. The congregation was evangelical,
though part of a mainline Presbyterian denomination. Their el-
ders decided to explicitly stipulate that no sexually active homosexual could be ordained as elder or deacon. My friend is a straight,
monogamous, married woman in her fifties. One of her two sons
is gay. She decided to resign her position because she did not feel
that she could, in good conscience, serve a church that her son
would view as yet another reason he had stopped identifying with
the faith he'd embraced in childhood.

One more story: I met a young man, John, who was debating a
crucial decision. John's father, a theologically and socially conservative Baptist minister, was dying of cancer. For years, John had
concealed his homosexual desires and involvements from his father. He found it very painful to think of his father dying without
ever having known what John considered an important aspect of
his identity. But John's brothers and sisters were begging him to
keep quiet. They did not want their father unnecessarily upset in
the short time he had to live. John was torn. Was it more loving to
talk with his father and trust his father's ability to respond or to
continue with silence? Which would John regret more—being

honest and possibly causing pain, or continuing the concealment that in his mind loomed as a chasm between his father and him?

HOMOSEXUALITY AND THE SIX LENSES

You have your own stories about divisions over issues surrounding homosexuality. Vivid disagreements do not happen only within the church. Our society at large is still deeply divided on issues related to sexual orientation—indeed, even over whether the term *sexual orientation* already stacks the deck in favor of one side or another of an acrimonious debate. Other terms, such as *sexual identity,* stack the deck too, with *sexual orientation* perhaps being more natural to the plain sex view, while *sexual identity* might be more at home in an expressive view.

These debates encompass issues that are intertwined but do not sort themselves neatly along the "conservative versus liberal" dichotomy so often presupposed in the media. A person might favor legalizing civil unions between gays but think that ordination of sexually active gays is incompatible with correct Christian doctrine. Another person might endorse ordination of gays, whether or not they are celibate, but oppose gay marriage blessed by the church.[1] The sexual lenses can help us diagnose some important dynamics of these debates.

We have already seen how differently the various lenses view sexuality in general. On the issue of homosexual practice, the procreative lens has a clear and consistent prescription: homosexual activity is impermissible because sexual organs are used in ways that cannot lead to procreation. Homosexual acts are sterile. Same-sex desires are disordered desires because sexual desire is designed to be expressed within monogamous, fruitful, lifelong unions, and homosexual unions can never be fruitful. Same-sex desires, then, should never be acted on. Those who have exclusively homosexual desires have a duty to be celibate unless they can reorient their desires.[2] Bisexuals (those who find themselves with both same-sex and opposite-sex attractions) will be coun-seled to find a partner of the opposite gender with whom they can form a happy marriage or to remain celibate.

This view of homosexuality is in stark contrast to that displayed in the August 16, 2010, "Back Story" section of *Newsweek* titled "How Long Will This Take?"[3] This feature displayed three time lines. One stretching from 1619 to the 2008 election of Barack Obama was labeled "Equal Rights for African-Americans." One stretching from 1826 to the 2010 appointment of Elena Kagan to the Supreme Court was labeled "Equal Rights for Women." And one stretching from the formation of the first national gay-rights organization in 1951 to 2010 was labeled "Equal Rights for Gays and Lesbians." The time lines all showed the herky-jerky history of referendums and voting results related to the three topics. The point of these juxtapositions is clear: progress takes time and set-backs are predictable, but eventually each of these "equal rights" struggles will have a triumphant ending. More specifically the piece predicts that gay marriage will be legalized in U.S. states eventually.

As we will soon see, it is from a romantic or expressive view, not from a procreative view, that advocacy for gay marriage looks like an equal rights struggle. The romantic and expressive views underlie many of the articles in the popular press about homo-sexuality. That 2010 piece echoed an essay called "The Loving De-cision" published in *Newsweek* soon after the 2008 national elec-tions.[4] Columnist Anna Quindlen's subject was the number of state ballot propositions aimed at outlawing gay marriage that had won voter approval. Her essay's title was intentionally ironic; her point was to display efforts to outlaw gay marriage as unloving.

Quindlen compared the laws enacted by these ballot measures to the antimiscegenation laws overturned by the Supreme Court in 1967. *Miscegenation* means racial mixing; up until 1967 several states still had laws making miscegenation a crime. It was illegal in many states for people of different races to marry. The Supreme Court's decision in *Loving v. Virginia* declared those laws unconstitutional.

Forty years later most citizens of the United States take for granted that it would be "connubial bigotry" (to use Quindlen's words) to deny the right of a man and a woman of two different races to marry. She hoped that four decades hence most U.S. citizens will see prohibitions on gay marriage as connubial bigotry. Quindlen called Mildred Loving, the black woman who was arrested for sleeping with her white husband, "an authority on battling connubial bigotry." In 2007, on the anniversary of the court's *Loving* decision, Mrs. Loving affirmed her belief that all Americans, "no matter their race, no matter their sex, no matter their sexual orientation, should have the same freedom to marry. That's what *Loving,* and loving, are all about."[5]

No one wants to be a bigot. To be a "bigot" is not just to be mistaken, but to be stubbornly and irrationally mistaken. Why does Quindlen think that all those who oppose gay marriage are "connubial bigots," on a par with those who deplored interracial marriage? Is she just being defamatory in order to score rhetorical points? Through what sexual lenses does such a view see sexuality?

Many of those who see the gay rights movement as parallel to the fight for racial equality see sexuality through either a romantic or an expressive lens. Viewed through the romantic lens, opposition to gay marriage looks irrational. After all, people often report having fallen in love with others of the same gender; why doubt their ability to tell whether this is so? If the purpose of sex is bodily consummation of romantic attachment, why would heterosexual love be the only appropriate foundation for an enduring commitment like marriage? Seen through the romantic lens, denying homosexual romantic love the same social support that society gives to heterosexual romantic love looks arbitrary and unloving.

The expressive lens makes opposition to gay sex look even more bigoted and problematic. Psychological research indicates that the orientation of people's sexual attraction lies along a spectrum.[6] Some women are attracted exclusively to men; some men are attracted only to women. Such people experience little or no attraction to those of their own gender. Bisexuals occupy the center of the spectrum, being attracted to both men and women. There is evidence that such people are relatively rare, a much smaller percentage than those at either end of the spectrum.[7] Some whose primary attractions are homosexual have some degree of attraction to those of the opposite gender. But there are people who experience *no* sexual attraction aside from same-sex attraction. Since expressivists see sexual expression as empowering and sexual restraint as likely to diminish or warp the self, they will see withholding the right to be sexually active, or the right to legally marry one's sexual partner if one chooses to do so, as restricting the ability to be fully human. From the expressive point of view there appears to be *no good reason* for denying sexual expression to those whose attractions are focused on those of their own gender. Hence the grounds for a charge like connubial bigotry.

But as obvious as the charge of connubial bigotry hurled at those who oppose gay marriage appears to romantics and expressivists, it looks completely unwarranted from a procreative view. And this is not just because no one likes to see himself as a bigot. The moral prescriptions given by the procreative view to homosexuals mirror the counsel given to heterosexuals: both are told to refrain from gratifying desires that they have toward partners who are not their spouse. This is consistency, not bigotry. And as long as someone is consistently applying the standards of the procreative view to all—heterosexuals and homosexuals alike—the charge of bigotry is unwarranted. As long as homosexual activity is seen as no more problematic than heterosexual extramarital sex, no more problematic than contraceptive sexual intercourse between spouses, no more problematic than masturbation, those who hold the procreative view are being both consistent and un-prejudiced. Even those who disagree with those who hold the pro-creative view should grant that at most they are mistaken. Bigots they are not.

Not all who oppose gay marriage or see homosexual activity as problematic adhere to the procreative view. Many individuals and groups with high visibility in the national debate make assertions affirming that God's design for sexual expression is between one man and one woman in the context of a lifelong, marital covenant. Some of these individuals and groups do not go on to endorse procreative positions on issues like the prohibition of contracep-tion within marriage. Does the covenantal lens, like the procre-ative lens, make gay marriage clearly impermissible?

Whether the covenantal view can allow for gay marriage is a matter of theological controversy among Protestants who see sex through the covenantal lens. Protestants who hold that the cove-nantal view requires a prohibition on monogamous same-sex unions cite at least four types of grounds for doing so. The first is the negative evaluation of homosexual activity expressed by vari-ous biblical writers and by many Christian theologians through-out history. Biblical passages often cited are Genesis 19; Leviticus 18:22 and 20:13; Judges 19; 1 Kings 14:24; 15:12; Romans 1:26-27; 1 Corinthians 6:9-10; 1 Timothy 1:9-10; Jude 1:7.

The second ground is a supposed slippery slope from monoga-mous gay marriage to polygamy: "If a man is allowed to marry another man, what will keep him from marrying two men—or three women? If marriage can mean anything, then it will mean nothing."[8] This concern seems rooted in the idea that once biblical strictures are overridden in one area of sexual conduct, there will be no grounds for complying with them in any other area.

The third ground is an assertion of gender complementarity. Males and females each bring unique and complementary qualities to sexuality and relationships. As theologian Richard B. Hays puts it, "Scripture affirms repeatedly that God has made man and woman for one another and that our sexual desires rightly find their fulfillment within heterosexual marriage."[9] He cites Mark 10:2-9; 1 Corinthians 7:1-9; Ephesians 5:21-33; 1 Thessalonians 4:3-8 and Hebrews 13:4 as evidence.

The fourth ground for covenantal prohibition of homosexual activity is based on the overarching narrative of Scripture about the significance of marriage. This overarching narrative includes, but is not exhausted by, gender complementarity. Two other aspects are noted by theologian Richard Hays.[10] First, this narrative implies that, since the Fall, humans are "slaves to sin" but that sin is still blameworthy. Many morally culpable acts are not under our voluntary control. This applies to homosexual desires and action no less than to other effects of fallen human nature. For these reasons, some theologians believe that even if homosexual orientation is involuntary, a biblical theological anthropology will not deem homosexual orientation to be morally neutral. A second aspect of this overarching biblical narrative is the demythologizing of sex. Scripture rejects the expressive view of sex. Scripture sees sexual fulfillment as only a subsidiary good—not even a close second to justice, mercy and faith. Taken as a whole, this overarching narrative about human sexuality entails that even though homosexuals may not be able to change their sexual desires, their desires (like many desires of heterosexuals) are disordered and need to be resisted. Celibacy is possible, albeit difficult for many. For conservatives with a covenantal view, celibacy for homosexuals is the only option endorsed by the biblical witness and nineteen centuries of theological reflection.

In contrast, however, other Christian theologians hold that the covenantal view is not incompatible with either monogamous gay marriage or ordination of practicing homosexuals. Arguments for this position are advanced by two different groups, with both groups finding alternative interpretations of the passages cited against homosexuality. They argue that many of these scriptural admonitions are on a par with kosher laws—valid only within a limited cultural context. One group of covenantal theologians holds that even though God's intended ideal for marriage is life-long heterosexual monogamy, merciful accommodations need to be made for those who cannot, for various reasons, approximate the ideal. Divorce is one such accommodation; allowing gay and lesbian unions is another. As theologian Allen D. Verhey puts it:

> If we allow divorce in a world like this for the sake of protect-ing marriage and marriage partners, then we must also con-sider allowing committed homosexual relationships for the sake of protecting fidelity and mutuality and the homosex-ual partners. It does not make either divorce or homosexual behavior a good. But it is still not yet the good future of God, and in a fallen world and a fallen sexuality, fidelity and mu-tuality can be a mark of God's good future.[11]

Such a view makes homosexual marriage no worse, but no better, than divorce.

Still others who hold the covenantal view think that treating gay marriage as an "accommodation" is still treating homosexuals as second-class humans. Theologian Alice Ogden Bellis thinks that it is possible, even likely, that if Jesus were alive today and a person were "caught" in a homosexual act within a monogamous gay union, Jesus would tell a parable of "the good homosexual" parallel to his famous story of the Good Samaritan. Because Jesus aligned himself with the outcasts of his day (Samaritans, tax collectors and women of questionable reputation), Bellis thinks that Jesus would seek to overturn cultural marginalization on the basis of sexual orienta-tion. Bellis maintains that "a positive attitude toward homosexual marriage . . . is not only consistent with Scripture but *mandated* by it,"[12] because of Scripture's concern for the marginalized.

Both of these groups of covenantal theologians believe that gay people should be encouraged to engage in covenant relationships; gay promiscuity is inappropriate in the same way that heterosexual promiscuity is.[13] Those who do not identify with Christianity will, understandably, have far less interest in how these debates unfold. But given the intricacies of the arguments marshaled on the various sides of these controversies, labeling those on the conservative end of these controversies as "connubial bigots" is unfair. It is an argumentative cheap shot that closes down dialogue, whether the charge comes from more liberal Christians or from secularists.

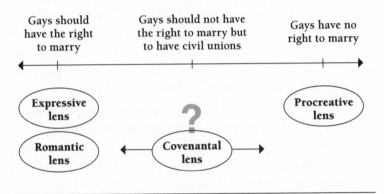

Figure 6

So far, our discussion makes the battle lines in the "culture wars" on issues concerning homosexual behavior look like they are drawn between the romantic, expressive, and some forms of the covenantal views (those that can be enlisted in support of gay marriage) on the one hand, and the procreative and other versions of the covenantal views (those that can be enlisted in opposition to gay marriage) on the other. What of the plain sex and power views?

The plain sex view endorses acting on one's sexual desires in ways that give personal pleasure and do not violate the rights of others. Sexual activity among consenting adult homosexuals will look unproblematic—even "natural"—through a plain sex lens. But the plain sex lens, in contrast to the romantic and expressive lenses, makes the fight for gays' marital rights look less than compelling. If sex is just about pleasure, then the pleasure of gay sex for those who are homosexual will be an important value to be weighed, though sexual activity will not be as central to the humanity of the participants as it seems to expressivists. It is doubtful that on the plain sex view monogamous marriage will be an important social institution—whether for heterosexuals or homosexuals.

Indeed, the plain sex view, not logically but psychologically, lends support to the anti-gay-marriage rhetoric of those who are "profamily." Recall the slippery-slope argument that we briefly considered above: "If a man is allowed to marry another man, why not two men or three women?" Why do so many profamily advocates fear that homosexual rights will undermine marriage? Perhaps because they make the unstated assumption that the main cultural competitor to the traditional covenantal or procreative views is the plain sex view. Most people, whether heterosexual or homosexual, have sexual desires that outstrip the boundaries of marriage. If one type of sexual desire—same-sex attraction—is given legal and social sanction, won't it be arbitrary to restrict marriage to only one partner? The plain sex view gives little or no reason not to act on desires for multiple partners. Hence, the plain sex view does seem to be a very weak foundation for monogamous marriage.

How and where the power lens is deployed in the discussion of homosexuality is a complex and contested issue. One use of power is in the rhetoric of argumentation. Another place where power becomes relevant is within gender dynamics. Anna Quindlen's term "connubial bigotry" is not a common term, though it may be more accurately descriptive than two more common terms in the debate over homosexuality. Those who think that homosexuals should be celibate are often accused of "homophobia" or "heterosexism." A phobia is an irrational fear. But often people are labeled homophobic on no more telling grounds than opposing gay marriage. Such people may have no fear of homosexuals, rational or otherwise, but merely disapprove of some of their behaviors. However, when people who view themselves as heterosexual seem disproportionately preoccupied with homosexuality and see restricting homosexual activity as an urgent imperative, it is worth asking why this, among all the pressing issues our society faces, seems so crucial to them. If their views do not seem to arise out of a coherent or defensible position, one might wonder whether they are looking hard at what is in another's eye in order to avoid coming to terms with what is in their own. Are they being judgmental? Are they being phobic? Perhaps.

But often, too, the term *homophobia* is used as a weapon to silence those whose views they dislike. If views are dismissed as homophobic, they need not be given the respect of intellectual examination and debate. So those who label others homophobic also need to examine their own motives and possible tendencies toward judgmentalism.

Heterosexism is an interesting term coined to point to dynamics that some feminists perceive through the power lens. According to the *Oxford English Dictionary,* this term was first used around 1979, in such contexts as, "Heterosexism designates, in particular, those central social structures which proscribe heterosexuality as the only 'natural' sexual interest."

Heterosexism draws a verbal parallel between prejudice against women and prejudice against homosexuals. Those who link feminist issues with gay rights push us to ask about terms like *effeminate,* a word that means "unmanly, feeble, overly refined." The term implies that men should not be like women because women are weak. In the past, *effeminate* was often used as a synonym for *male homosexual* but was also often used to express distaste for men who did not fit certain gender stereotypes about what "real men" should be like. To be tough, competitive, uninterested in the arts, was manly. To be gentle, relational or artistic was "womanish" or effeminate. Could prejudice against gay men have similar roots to prejudice against women? Feminists like Suzanne Pharr think so. She asserts, for example, "Many heterosexual women see [a lesbian] as someone who stands in contradiction to the sacrifices they have made to conform to compulsory heterosexuality," and "visible gay men are the objects of extreme hatred and fear by heterosexual men because their breaking ranks with male heterosexual solidarity is seen as a damaging rent in the very fabric of sexism."[14] Such views have led some feminists to maintain that consistent feminism requires advocacy for gay, lesbian, bisexual and transsexual rights. Some radical feminists go further, arguing that patriarchy and oppression of women are so entwined with heterosexual male power that the only way for women to be fully liberated is to live entirely apart from men. While not all lesbians are feminists and only a minority of feminists are lesbians, some radical feminists have advocated lesbianism as a political choice. Hence the slogan, "feminism is the theory; lesbianism is the practice."[15]

"Connubial bigotry." "Marriage Protection Act." "Down with Heterosexism." "Save the Family." "A Woman Without a Man Is Like a Fish Without a Bicycle." Slogans are easy. Sorting out the arguments is much harder work. Knowing what lenses we are using can help. So can listening with patience before we label others or dismiss their views.

LIVING FAITHFULLY WHILE DISAGREEING

Why do Christians disagree about a matter central to living out the Christian life—either their own life or the lives of others who claim the name of Christ? When talking about literal phoropters at the beginning of this book, we saw that when lenses are dropped into place, what matters is not just the particular combination of lenses, but how they are rotated. We have also seen that the covenantal lens is seldom deployed in isolation (nor should it be, if my argument in chapter two is cogent). The differences concerning gay marriage among theologians, all of whom consider themselves to be expounding a covenantal perspective, are due to nuances of textual interpretation, but these interpretations may in turn be influenced by how other lenses (be those power or romantic or expressive) are being combined with the covenantal lens as they look intently at the evidence. What looks like finally having arrived at orthophoria with the aid of twentieth-century biology and psychology to some more "liberal" covenantal theologians looks like revisionist heterophoria to others. What looks like faithful orthodoxy to some "conservative" covenantal theologians looks like fearful and brittle myopia to others. Where do you perceive orthophoria on this issue to reside?

Could God have brought it about that those who sincerely seek God's will would all come to the same conclusion on central human issues? We see ourselves and others in a mirror dimly; I often find human life a riddle. God has also not brought it about that sincere Christians thinking hard and prayerfully might converge on a shared confidence in knowing God's mind on this (and many other issues).

Is dimness on this issue and other issues a result of the Fall? Or is this a disguised blessing? Could our divergence of perspectives become a resource for Christian discipleship? When you love those who love you, what credit is that to you? When you love those who share your views on matters you think central to the faith, what credit is that to you? You don't need grace for *that*. We do need grace and mercy and wisdom, and a life saturated with prayerful seeking, to live out our life together in light of our very real disagreements.

I've often thought about the parable of the prodigal son as a story that is meant to enrich our compassion for God. When the prodigal returns, his elder brother exits the house as the father prepares the welcome feast. How does a father feel when he cannot keep his sons both living in the same house, having the same celebration? Will a shared eternity of enjoying God be possible for all those whom God longs to have fellowship with if we cannot love one another and be in fellowship despite our differences? The kingdom of heaven is a realm in which all those present can be unconditionally joyful about sharing the same "space." Can we Christians take baby steps to being able to do that here on earth? Can those of us who think we know God's will on this matter speak that truth in loving ways that are not themselves arrogant or dismissive of alternative views? Can those of us who find this issue profoundly confusing continue to seek wisdom rather than avoiding hard questions and issues? Aren't we obliged to take such steps by our praying as Jesus taught us to pray: "Your kingdom come; your will be done, *on earth as it is in heaven*"?

PART FOUR

Convolutions—
A World Shaped by
Deficient Visions

Casual Sex

Sara told me the story around bouts of tears. She had met Mark on Facebook a month before their first semester of college. Sara loved country music. Mark's Facebook page showed him wearing a cowboy hat, tilted at just the angle used by her favorite singer. Neither of them knew many people at the college they planned to attend, so they'd been happy to find one another through a social network. They had had several extended e-mail conversations before they arrived on campus. Sara was eager to talk with him in person.

Mark arranged to meet at her dorm during the first week of classes. He was even cuter than his photos, though a bit shorter than she'd imagined. They went for a stroll across campus and through the nearby city park. They sat on a bench and watched the squirrels. Mark didn't talk much, but that seemed in keeping with his cowboy image. Eventually Mark suggested that they go get his pickup truck and explore the nearby community. As they drove his hand brushed her knee each time he shifted gears. They found a place where they could watch the sun set over the lake.

Mark draped his arm around her shoulder, and they began kissing. Mark was a good kisser, and she was more than enjoying herself. After the windows fogged up, he took a condom out of his back pocket and set it on the dashboard. She looked at him and said, "Mark, we are not going to have sex." But she didn't ask to leave and continued to return his kisses and caresses with passion. As he started to remove her clothes she again said, "We're not having sex." But they did have sex, and now, a week later, he hadn't emailed, hadn't called, and had even ignored her the three times their paths crossed on campus. She felt awful. Sara was angry at Mark and disgusted with herself.

Her roommate told her to toughen up. "This is college. Hookups happen all the time. Grow up. Learn from this. Move on."

Hooking Up, Casual Sex and Promiscuity

Hookup, I've learned from conversations with college students, is a term designed to be ambiguous and neutral. "I hooked up with that person you saw me leave the party with," could mean as little as "We did some passionate kissing" or it could mean "We had sexual intercourse." Hookups are noncommittal, sexualized exchanges where sexual intercourse may or may not be involved. *Hookup* also conveys that sexual exchanges, whatever the details, are no big deal.

For many in our culture casual sex is seen as a significant source of pleasure. They may have a "bad date" now and then, but quite often their sexual encounters bring them both personal pleasure and the satisfaction of having given someone else pleasure. Christians who have internalized a covenantal or procreative view of sexuality can find this puzzling and disturbing. They can make sense of what has gone wrong for Sara, but they don't know how to address someone like Russell Vannoy, for example, who asserts that sex unencumbered with love is better sex.[1] Impersonal sex, Vannoy and others imply, is less complicated and allows for concentrating on skill, sensation and mutual pleasure. This sort of plain sex person wants sex to be not just plain but impersonal.

As we have seen, we live in a culture where people look at sex through contrasting lenses. The Christian tradition holds that in the beginning sex was sacred and intended to cement a monogamous, lifelong union between a man and a woman, but that human sinfulness all too often distorts sexuality, making it destructive or trivial. Many others within our culture hold an alternative narrative about sex. In the beginning, so this story goes, sex was a natural human appetite. However, because sexual intercourse led to pregnancy, males who wanted to reliably identify their offspring wanted their mates to be sexually monogamous. So there was enormous pressure for women to remain chaste until marriage. Virginity in women was valued; women who were willing to have sex outside of marriage were unlikely to find men who would financially support them and their children. But once reliable contraception was invented, sex could be separated from reproduction. It became rational to seek as much sexual satisfaction as one could get with willing partners.

Historically, pragmatic warnings against casual sex have been based on the dangers of unplanned pregnancy and sexually transmitted diseases. The plain sex view would emphasize that negative consequences are only part of the picture, and a shrinking element at that. Concerns about pregnancy and disease are challenges that can be effectively overcome by "safe sex." Concerns about the guilt and shame that extramarital sex produces will be viewed as bogus by plain sex sorts. If sex is just a significant source of pleasure, if people are honest with one another, "on the same page" and all that, then what is there to feel guilty about?

Both casual sex and hooking up are at home in this plain sex narrative. *Casual sex* is a term that has been around longer than *hooking up*. It has a similar meaning: noncommittal sexual activity between people who are aware of each other's lack of commitment and share one another's attitude toward their uncommitted sexual involvement. But casual sex covers a varied mix of sexual intentions. Casual sex can mean "recreational sex"—being out for a good time. Casual sex can be making do with what's available to feed an appetite—the equivalent of fast food. Casual sex can mean being "friends with benefits"—two people who know and like one another but have no serious intention of sustaining a relationship and who may have no romantic feelings, but sleep together as a convenience. Casual sex can also be desperate sex—seeking out a partner, any partner, out of neediness or loneliness or unsatisfied sexual craving. For some, casual sex is a way of getting to know someone better—not quite like a handshake or hug or extended conversation, but close. And for some others, casual sex is "scoring"—putting a notch on one's belt, making a conquest, proving one's attractiveness to others.

Christians tend to consider all casual sex promiscuity. Seen through the plain sex lens, *promiscuous* seems a quaint word—a term that flags its user as prim and the person they are talking about as tarnished. Yet many people who have multiple sexual partners would not see themselves as promiscuous. Rather they see themselves as having standards and living up to them. Their code of ethics differs from the traditional strictures of the covenantal or procreative views, but they do live by a sexual ethic.

ETHICS AND CASUAL SEX
Understanding how the world looks to such people necessitates looking at casual sex with more equipment than the six sexual lenses of our "phoropter." This is because there are ethical disputes among all people who use a plain sex lens. These disputes often arise because differing ethical "lenses" are combined with the plain sex lens in evaluating sexual conduct. At other times, the same ethical lens is being used by various disputants, but some of them are using a romantic or expressive lens, not a plain sex one.

So we need a bit more understanding about ethical theories.

Ethics is a collection of evaluations of conduct or character based on what human beings, as such, should be and do. Ethical evaluations are based on what human beings, as such, are owed. There are, of course, significant disagreements about the content of ethics—about what we do owe one another and about what sorts of people we should strive to be. Christians naturally base their ethical views on a biblical anthropology. But, as we saw in chapters two and five, Christians often disagree with one another about the implications of theological anthropology. And Christians often find significant common moral ground with adherents of other religions and with principled secularists.

We are heirs to twenty-five hundred years of vital conversation about the nature and content of ethics. For our purposes, it is useful to simplify the content of that two-millennium-long conversation down to three main approaches to ethics that are most used by current academic philosophers: virtue-oriented ethics, duty-oriented ethics and consequence-oriented ethics. Combining these three lenses with the sexual lenses we already have in our "Phoropter" will help us sharpen our sexual insight and help us sort out the ethical spectrum occupied by those in our society that do not hold a covenantal or procreative view of sexuality.

We've already commented extensively on virtue-oriented ethics in discussing the virtue of chastity in chapter three, but we only touched briefly on duty-oriented and consequence-oriented approaches. As we examine issues surrounding casual sex, these latter two approaches become more relevant.

Duty-oriented ethical views focus on evaluations of actions based on asking what obligations I have to act in certain ways or to refrain from acting in other ways. A parent, for example, has obligations to support and nurture his or her children. A parent who has food but who withholds the food from his or her child is falling short of a particular duty of parenthood. We also have ways of binding ourselves to particular future obligations. In general, I do not have an obligation to give money to any particular charity, but if I promise to contribute $100 to Habitat for Humanity, then by promising I have created a duty to contribute.

There are certain important duties that we have to all people, no matter what our other relationships are to them. Uncontroversial duties of this kind are duties not to wantonly kill or harm others. Many people also think that we have duties to help those who are in desperate need, especially if we can do so with little cost to ourselves. Calling 911 when we see someone being attacked outside our window would be an example of such a duty of beneficence.

The eighteenth-century philosopher Immanuel Kant has had enormous influence on duty-oriented philosophical ethics. The focus of Kant's approach is on the claim that human nature, as such, demands ethical respect. Respect for humanity sets limits on what we can do—even in cases where acting in a particular way would bring about many good things. The main principle of Kantianism, called the Categorical Imperative, is stated in various ways. One memorable version is, "Always act in accord with policies of actions that treat humanity, whether in yourself or another, as an end in itself and never as a mere means."[2] When I threaten someone with bodily harm in order to get him to give me his money, I am using him as a means to becoming richer. I ignore that he may be prevented from pursuing projects that he values because I have taken money he may need. I treat him and his projects as if they have no value. This is certainly not treating him as an end in himself.

Jeremy Bentham and John Stuart Mill, two British philosophers who were also active in social reform in the eighteenth and nineteenth centuries, championed the idea that judgments of right and wrong must be based on the outcomes of our actions.[3] Their consequence-oriented ethic is called Utilitarianism. The main principle of ethics on this view is, "Always act so that you maximize the pleasure and minimize the pain of all those affected by your actions." Utilitarians do not dispute that we have, for example, duties to feed our children or duties to keep promises. However, they think that the foundation of these duties lies in the fact that parental obligations and promise keeping decrease suffering and contribute to human well-being. Moreover, they hold that "hard cases" where duties conflict need to be settled by appeal to the Principle of Utility. If I have promised to meet someone for lunch at a particular time but pass someone in need of immediate assistance, keeping my promise out of a sense of duty would be an ethical mistake. Utilitarianism is a prominent form of consequence-oriented ethics, but it is not the only form. Utilitarians believe that all good consequences can ultimately be reduced to pleasure and all bad consequences can ultimately be reduced to pain.[4]

As we saw with virtue-oriented ethics, duty-oriented and consequence-oriented approaches also have had both secular and religious proponents. Kant and Mill both thought of themselves as offering an interpretation of "the Golden Rule of Jesus of Nazareth": Do unto others as you would have done unto you. What would Jesus do? According to Kant, Jesus would treat each person as an end and not a mere means. According to Mill, Jesus would ensure that pain and suffering were minimized and happiness was available to all. At the same time, both Kant and Mill developed their theories as ways of avoiding having to settle theological disputes before arriving at ethical agreement. Atheists, agnostics, Christians and adherents of other theistic religions will find it very difficult to agree on whether God has issued commands and what the content of those commands are. They may find it much easier to start with a shared sense that humanity is owed respect or that pain should be minimized.

Christians hold that ethics is not enough to ensure a well-lived human life—to live well we need grace and ultimate fulfillment in fellowship to God. Yet ethics can be an arena in which Christians and people of other faiths or of no faith can find common ground. While Christians are going to see casual sex as falling short of God's intentions for sexuality, seeing how these various ethical theories apply to casual sex can at least help us understand that many non-Christians are striving to operate with varying degrees of integrity even while engaging in casual sex.

ETHICS AND RAPE

With these ethical theories in mind, let's think harder about Mark and Sara's encounter above. Sara is clearly unhappy; was she wronged? In the process of her research for *Sex and the Soul,* Donna Freitas was disturbed by the number of young women who "recounted being raped without calling it that." One story she tells is Julia's, who had told her high school boyfriend repeatedly that she didn't want to have sex with him. Julia tells Freitas, "I told him I didn't want to do it, but I don't feel like he raped me, but it *was* against my will the first time. I don't really know all the definitions of those types of things."[5]

Rape is wrong—seriously wrong. If there is one ethical claim about sexual conduct that is uncontroversial, this must be it. Consequence-oriented theories will see rape as wrong because it causes much, much more pain for its victim than could ever be counterbalanced by the pleasure of the perpetrator. Duty-oriented theories will see rape as a violation of bodily integrity; rape violates the need each human being has to control what happens in and to our body. Virtue-oriented theories will see rape as a product of such vices as brutality, cruelty, self-absorption and lack of compassion.

The wrongness of rape seems clear no matter which sexual lens one combines with these ethical lenses. If, viewed through the starkest versions of the power lens, rape's wrongness seems doubtful, then it would be more reasonable to condemn the starkest version of the power lens as immoral rather than to reconsider the ethics of rape. The Marquis de Sade argued that he, and all other men who were strong enough to overpower any woman, had "incontestable rights to the enjoyment of her; I have the right to force from her this enjoyment, if she refuses me it for whatever the cause may be."[6] But these views have made de Sade synonymous with immoralism and infamous for it.

Subjecting someone to nonconsensual sexual involvement can be shown to be impermissible on both consequentialist and duty-oriented accounts. First, being co-opted into nonconsensual sex is almost never pleasant (indeed, it is often physically painful and psychologically traumatizing). Since in the plain sex view the central good of sexual desire and sexual behavior is pleasure, initiating or continuing nonconsensual sex undermines the central good of sex and is, therefore, wrong. Second, expressivists will note that sex is a mutual disclosure in circumstances of particular intimacy and vulnerability. Duty-oriented ethics will hold that humans are entitled to regulate access to their own bodies. So failures to respect this right to bodily integrity violate an important duty humans owe to one another.

Rape is wrong. Uncontroversial. But what is rape? The paradigm case of rape is a stranger who uses force or the threat of violence to make an unwilling victim have intercourse. But as sexual encounters between people who know one another only casually became more widespread, "What is date rape?" became an urgent question. That question cannot be answered without a careful examination of sexual consent.

THE ETHICAL IMPORTANCE OF SEXUAL CONSENT

In the early 1990s, Antioch College got a lot of press for enacting a formal policy requiring explicit verbal consent to sexual acts. The stated intent of the policy was to make date rape less likely and to improve communication. Such policies make good sense through the plain sex lens, where sex is about seeking, achieving and giving pleasurable sensations. What specific sexual practices are engaged in, and under what circumstances, seems a matter appropriately defined by the terms of the participants' agreement, under the important assumption that all involved are willing participants in the activity.

Philosopher David Archard's book *Sexual Consent* explores many of the complexities of consent.[7] Consent is an important moral consideration no matter which sexual lens one is using, even though those with a covenantal, procreative or romantic view will think that other considerations beside consent (commitment, for example) are morally relevant.

Make sure that there is consent is not a simple rule to follow. Consent is complicated by the ambiguous borders between persuasion and coercion, as we saw in chapter four in discussing flirtation and seduction. Consent is also complicated by such factors as age differences, power dynamics, and the murky role of alcohol and drugs in sexual encounters.

Consent is an act rather than a state of mind. If consent is an act, it needs to be *given;* it should not simply be assumed in the absence of any sign to the contrary. Lack of a "No" is not equivalent to a "Yes." This means that it is a mistake to infer consent to sexual activities from the absence of an explicit "No."

Lots of people made fun of Antioch College's *Sexual Offense Prevention Policy* because of its demand that consent be both explicit and specific: "Can I put my hand here?" "Can I remove your shirt?" Critics asked, "Isn't all that talk awkward and artificial? Don't people naturally move from one thing to another within a sexual encounter?" But Antioch College was trying to help students avoid painful sexual misunderstandings.[8]

Sexual misunderstandings arise when one person assumes that either tacit or indirect consent is given to some activity—but the other person makes no such assumption. After a sexual encounter one person might say, "What do you mean you didn't want to have sex; why'd you invite me up to your room then?" "What do you mean I should have stopped? Anyone who goes in for . . . obviously is willing to . . ." Mark thought that Sara wanted sex because she was willing to engage in passionate kissing in an isolated spot. He thought she was just being coy when she said, "We're not having sex." She didn't kiss like someone who wanted to stop. His failure to stop caused real harm. This shows how dangerous the idea of tacit and indirect consent can be.

Tacit means without verbal articulation. Tacit consent, when it exists, is part of an unexpressed mutual understanding. Certainly there are many other areas where an assumption of tacit consent is reasonable. For example, a student assumes that the instructor is giving tacit consent to the student's continuing to work on a test after the official end of the class period if the instructor has not told students that they must stop working and turn in their tests.

Indirect consent is when a person consents to one thing by consenting to something else. When I, for example, answer the waitperson's "Can I take your order?" by saying, "Yes, I'll have a shrimp salad," I am consenting *directly* to having her bring me a salad and *indirectly* to paying the bill at the end of the meal.

Archard's *Sexual Consent* makes the important point that tacit consent and indirect consent only work when there is a firm, clear and widely shared agreement about the conventions governing a form of behavior. Tacit agreements work in sports, for example, because players know the rules that define the game and, by participating, implicitly agree to abide by the rules of the game. Indirect consent rests on similar social "rules," as in the restaurant case where the customer indirectly consents to being charged the stated price at the end of the meal. "But I never explicitly said I'd pay the bill" will not get you anywhere in such a setting.

Both tacit and indirect consent rest on shared understandings and social conventions. However, given the array of sexual subcultures within our society, each with differing lenses, there are no widely shared conventions. This explains why assumptions of tacit and indirect consent in sexual encounters have caused much misunderstanding and harm. If one person assumes that consent to passionate kissing constitutes indirect consent to sexual intercourse, but the other person makes no such assumption, sexual assault is all too likely to occur. If one person assumes that not saying no is the same thing as consenting to an escalated level of sexual intimacy, and the other makes no such assumption, harmful misunderstanding is a likely consequence. For these reasons, it is wrong to rely on risky and uncertain convention when verbal clarification can avoid serious harm.

One very common myth underwriting belief in indirect sexual consent is that male arousal has a "point of no return." This is the assumption that in sexual activity and arousal there is a point beyond which escalating arousal cannot be halted short of intercourse and (male) climax. One especially sad part of the story that opened this chapter was that, when Sara asked Mark why he didn't stop when she said no, he responded, "A man can only think with one head at a time."

The myth of a point of no return is dangerous because it shifts the burden of responsibility for nonconsensual sex onto women. But a consequentialist account can show that a woman has a right to withdraw her consent and call a halt to sexual intimacy at every stage—even after penetration has occurred. This is because "a man can desist from intercourse at little or no cost to himself" while "the costs to a woman of unconsented sex are considerable."[9] Consent is needed for each heightened level of sexual intimacy up to and including intercourse.

Explicit consent is, of course, not usually sought or given in established and stable sexual relationships. Sexual partners who know one another well commonly communicate their desires through gestures that are understood against the backdrop of shared past experiences. Tacit consent does have an appropriate place within such relationships, yet even such relationships are not beyond the need for consent. Having consented to sexual intercourse in the past does not constitute indirect consent to any and all future sexual encounters with the same partner. Consent (whether tacit or explicit) is necessary nonetheless.

It is within the realm of casual sex that explicit sexual consent is most ethically important. Yet a standard worry, perhaps especially among men, is that people will be falsely accused of having engaged in nonconsensual sex when in fact the sex was, at most, regrettable. People do sometimes consent to sex and wish later that they had not.

Not long ago I noticed that an enterprising person was selling a solution to this worry on eBay. One could buy a stack of "sexual consent cards," which had a place for the signature of the parties and could be used to spell out explicitly, and in writing, what the terms of the sexual encounter were. Insisting that one's partner sign such a card might betoken a certain lack of trust, but such a lack of trust might not be out of place when engaging in "plain sex" with a virtual stranger, or even with an acquaintance. Using sexual consent cards might be more than a little awkward, but such a practice does apply due diligence toward preventing harmful sexual misunderstandings.

But explicit verbal consent—even written consent—is not all that is morally necessary. It is very important to distinguish between mere verbal agreement and *valid* consent. A child cannot validly consent to sex if below the age when he or she can understand and appreciate both the biological facts of sex and what having sex means. So immaturity invalidates consent. Fraud and coercion are other conditions that invalidate consent; so does intoxication.

Ogden Nash became well-known in the twentieth century for writing catchy and humorous short poems. One Nash poem, titled "Reflections on Ice-Breaking," reads,

Candy
Is dandy,
But liquor
Is quicker.[10]

Nash was writing in a cultural context where men routinely sent women small presents—flowers and candy—while "courting" them as part of a ritual that officially aspired to transition from romance to covenant to procreation. Little girls in this era skipped rope to chants like "First comes love, then comes marriage, then comes Sally with a baby carriage." Nash's poem makes the wry and somewhat cynical point that wooing a woman by sending her small presents like candy might eventually lead to sexual intimacy, but if you want to speed things along, get her drunk. Before the term *date rape* was invented, this poem counted as funny.

Is Casual Sex Ethical?
A Debate Among the Lenses

Consent is an important moral requirement. And when combining a plain sex lens with a duty-oriented or consequence-oriented ethic, it may look like the only moral requirement. But though expressivists will not see the importance of commitment in the same way that the covenantal, procreative and romantic lenses will, expressivists will seek more than consensual sex. Expressivist Seiriol Morgan notes that sex is not just bodily but also "in the head." Because of this we need to take into account the "intentional content" of sexual desire (that is, what the desire triggers and conveys imaginatively). What the participants are feeling and thinking while they are sexually engaged deserves evaluation from an ethical point of view as much as what they are doing with their own and another's body. Sometimes what sex expresses, and is intending to express, is eroticized contempt, eroticized domination, eroticized misogyny and narcissistic delight in seducing someone. These intentional contents are, according to Morgan, so morally problematic that no amount of consent can make their satisfaction morally permissible. In fact, consenting to be party to their imaginative enactment may itself be morally impermissible.[11]

Morgan's point applies a Kantian duty-oriented principle of human respect across the array of sexual lenses we have been considering. Naomi Wolf remembers an interesting example of the power view of sexuality from her college days: "some fraternities had a designated urinal above which the guys were supposed to put individual pubic hairs of girls they had seduced."[12] Is sex still casual if "scoring" and scorekeeping are the point and intent of one of its participants?

Both partners may have a shared understanding regarding "no strings" to an encounter, but one of them might still be extremely uncomfortable with having her (or his) pubic hair become part of a trophy collection. The consequential ethical lens would urge taking into account any pain upon finding out one had been a number on a scorecard as a reason against pursuing sex with such intent. The duty-oriented lens would, at minimum, urge transparency—disclosing not just one's lack of commitment but one's trophy-collecting goals as well. And a virtue-oriented lens would see such intent as callous and crude. In short, all three ethical lenses would fit uncomfortably with so-called casual sex as a competitive sport.

Wolf herself is torn. She sees some ways the Sexual Revolution, which made casual sex much more socially acceptable, has given women more freedom than they had in what she calls "the bad old days of enforced virginity." But she also says, "There is a terrible spiritual and emotional hunger among many women, including myself, for social behavior and ritual that respect and even worship female sexuality and reproductive power. We are no longer—

if we ever really were—goddesses, priestesses, or queens of our own sexuality. But we want to be."[13]

Expressivists differ over whether sexual vareity is an important value. An interesting exchange on this subject took place in the mid-1970s between philosophers Robert Solomon and Janice Moulton. In his article "Sexual Paradigms" Solomon claimed that sex with new partners is *better sex* because two people who are just getting to know one another sexually will have much more to say to one another. In contrast, he claims that couples who have been together for years "have probably been repeating the same messages for years" and their body language has likely become "abbreviated ritual incantations of the lengthy conversations they had years before."[14] Janis Moulton disputes Solomon's characterization, pointing out that if sex really is body language, then casual sex is likely to be trite in comparison with sex within a long-term relationship, just as party chitchat with virtual strangers is thin in comparison with a heart-to-heart talk with someone whom we know well.[15]

In order to avoid both shallowness and exploitation, clarity about levels of commitment and the imaginative meanings is a vital prelude to sexual encounters. One fairly recent study of seventeen- to twenty-year-olds showed that young women were more likely to see their sexual encounters as happening within steady or committed relationships. In other words, these young women do not see themselves as engaging in casual sex. Yet the study showed that young men viewed "what must be essentially the same encounters as casual."[16]

Loosely defined serial monogamy has become a common pattern for adolescent sexual relationships. If "we'll be monogamous until we choose to see other people" is not ultimately a committed relationship, the male perception of these relationships as casual is more descriptively accurate. The young women are seeing the relationships as committed (perhaps because they hope that they

are or will become committed), but more often, as things tran-
spire, these relationships turn out to be short-term.[17]

Defenders of casual sex may point out that not everyone has a
choice between casual sex and a long-term relationship. Some
people go for years without finding someone to whom they want
to commit and with whom that feeling is mutual. A person may
not be *seeking* shallow relationships, but that may be all he or she
is *finding* at the moment.

Won't casual sex be seen through both the plain sex and the
expressive lenses as both permissible and as far better than no sex
at all? Proponents of plain sex often draw an analogy with hunger
and eating—a gourmet meal in a fine dining establishment is better by far than fast food, but if one is hungry and fast food is the
only available food, it would be foolish to pass up the opportunity
to satisfy an important human need.[18] Expressivists might make a
similar point with a different analogy. Chitchat isn't as good as
deep conversation, but chitchat is better than going for long, long
stretches with no one to talk to at all.

Some of those using the plain sex or expressive lenses see casual sex as permitted (perhaps in a pinch) without recommending
it.[19] But indulging in casual sex has a high potential cost. Philosopher John Hunter points out the danger here: "If we sometimes
make love when there is not affection or personal delight being
expressed, then even when we are with someone for whom we
care, the spell may be broken and our intimacies may remain private pleasures happening to require the cooperation of another
person." As Hunter points out, "the significance that we can at-
tach to sexual activity . . . is a magic and a fragile thing."[20]

For a significant number of people in modern Western culture,
casual sex is viewed as a phase one goes through. For some, a period in which they have a series of casual sexual encounters is
followed by "settling down" to a committed sexual relationship.[21]
Many people think that their sexual lives will unfold like this: "I

will have casual sex until I find someone I care about deeply and who cares about me deeply too—with whom I want to be personally intimate as well as sexually intimate. Sex then will become an expression of deep care and affection for one particular person. We'll become exclusive, a couple. Casual sex will then become inappropriate for both of us unless we break up. If this goes on long enough, it will make sense for us to make a permanent (or at least long-term) commitment to one another." Plain sex will morph into romantic sex, which will morph into covenantal sex.

Icelandic philosopher Kristjan Kristjansson thinks that these expectations ignore that human beings are creatures of habit—"most of our personal characteristics arise through repeated practice."[22] Our actions form our character and attitudes. Casual sex habituates us to focus on other people as replaceable collections of qualities—as sexually attractive bodies. In contrast, loving sex focuses on another person as irreplaceable, cultivating an enduring and time-intensive commitment to the whole person. Another person with a similar body would not be loved sexually by someone who genuinely loved another. Repeated casual sex encounters undermine our ability to form a "deep relationship with a single other."[23] It is unreasonable to expect that one can have sex as fancy dictates and opportunity allows but also hope that some of the time sex is combined with personal intimacy. Through Kristjannson's virtue-oriented lens the coherence and wisdom of seeing casual sex as a phase that would later give way to "settling down" looks questionable. If casual sex habituates us to see others as replaceable, then it is doubtful that a practitioner of casual sex can become, at will, someone who is capable of combining love and deep commitment with sex. It is unlikely that sexual lenses will work like sunglasses—they cannot be put on or removed at will.

Before leaving the topic of casual sex, we should take one more look at casual sex through the duty-oriented lens. Above we said that the duty-oriented lens would, *at minimum,* urge full disclosure of motives when engaging in sexual intercourse. It will be remembered that one important ethicist who emphasized duty was Immanuel Kant. When Kant applied his Categorical Imperative to the area of sexuality, he argued that treating humanity as an end in itself, not as a mere means, required much more than honesty and a shared understanding. While Kristjannson was concerned that repeatedly engaging in casual sex would habituate us to focus on other people as replaceable collections of qualities, Kant thought that doing this *even one time* disrespects not only the humanity of one's partner but one's own humanity as well. Two people stimulating and satisfying one another's desires are just using one another as a mere means. Kant puts it this way: "Their object is not human nature but sex, and each of them dishonors the human nature of the other."[24] Kant further asserts, "A man cannot make of his person a thing."[25]

Sometimes commentators have implied that Kant was antisex. But he was just anti-non-marital sex. Kant argued that the right to make sexual use of someone else requires a right over their whole person. The only way that this would not be degrading is if it were mutual. "If I yield myself completely to another and obtain the person of the other in return, I win myself back."[26] Many modern Kantians have not wanted to go this far with Kant, arguing instead that treating someone as an end requires only refraining from coercing, deceiving or manipulating him or her. However, Kant's position should not be lightly dismissed. In essence he is arguing that the duty-oriented lens of the Categorical Imperative is compatible only with the covenantal and procreative sexual lenses. Kant's philosophical stature should not coerce our assent to his position, but it should lead us to give his argument due consideration.

SEX AS A COMMODITY

Before class one day, two of my students were talking about a rock concert they had attended over the weekend. They guessed that the preevent entertainment raised issues pertinent to our Sexual Ethics course, but were not sure what to think about it. The concert had been held in a sports arena. As people made their way in, women were invited to bare their breasts for broadcast on the Jumbotron.

"Why would anyone do that?" I asked.

They shrugged. "No one thinks it's a big deal."

The layers of irony here are apparent. The official party line that makes displaying your breasts on the Jumbotron "no big deal" is the plain sex lens. But this form of entertainment is all about power. Some of the young women who put themselves on display may see themselves as empowered. They may think they are freely choosing to express their sexuality. And if a woman's "rack" gets more applause than the last one, she may get an ego boost. But other women may feel pressured to go along—fearful of seeming prudish or insecure. More importantly, what's happening has as much to do with men as with female competition. The standards of comparison here are set by male eyes, even when women are looking. And the real winners are the concert organizers. They have revved up the crowd without having to cut into their phenomenal profit margin.

A recent book by Susan J. Douglas calls the phenomenon at work here "enlightened sexism."[1] Enlightened sexism claims that, now that society has become "enlightened" about women's rights, women have arrived—women have gained economic and social equality with men. The story continues by adding that now a woman can "have it all," meaning not just career success and a happy family, if she wants one, but the freedom to use her body and her sexuality to get men to lust after her. Enlightened sexism celebrates the empowerment of women; sometimes even touting "girl power" as a new version of feminism. Women supposedly can exert power in the boardroom *and* keep their figure sleek by going to pole-dancing class in the evening. Hillary Clinton by day; sex kitten by night. But the underpinnings of enlightened sexism are actually exploitive commercialism. Enlightened sexism allowed those who came up with the concept for the *Girl's Gone Wild* videos to produce "soft" pornographic footage while keeping their overhead costs at bargain-basement levels. Enlightened sexism also underlies a lot of reality TV, as well as the music industry, beauty industry, diet industry and fashion merchandising.

Susan Douglas is surely on target in much of her analysis. Yet the commercialization of sexuality is an equal-opportunity exploiter in many ways. Abercrombie and Fitch has certainly succeeded in objectifying the male torso and abdominals. Ads for the "little blue pill" are ubiquitous on both network and cable television. Every man wants to be "ready" when the "time is right." And the subject headings of the dreck captured by my e-mail spam filter are revealing. Those profiting from male performance anxiety are focusing on more than readiness. Men also are urged to worry about size and stamina. "Add inches" and "Go all night" are two of the headings polite enough to be noted here.

The power lens helps us stand back from the hype and ask questions. Yet, on its own, the power lens doesn't provide much guidance. What are the procreative and covenantal lenses to make of all this? Should Christians never shop at Victoria's Secret or take Viagra? How can we resist the exploitive objectification of the human body while still admiring the expressiveness of the nude in art?

I suggest that we will be better equipped to pursue such questions after an excursion through debates among those whom I've called principled secularists. The value that both the covenantal and procreative views place on chastity underwrites clear prohibitions on participation in activities that commercialize sex— namely, prostitution and pornography.[2] These prohibitions are so clear that those who view sex through these lenses often don't have much to tell us beyond "Just say no." The murkier territory that prostitution and pornography represent for other lenses has led to heated debates. In turn, these debates have produced both flimsy rationalizations and useful insights. Sorting wheat from chaff among those who see sex through the power, plain sex and expressive lenses will yield insights that the covenantal view can endorse while also helping us understand how principled secularists think about these matters.

The Plain Sex Lens and Prostitution

Through the plain sex lens, prostitution and pornography have very similar moral contours. The salient issues from a plain sex point of view are autonomy, consent and maximizing sexual pleasure.

A significant number of those who view sex through the plain sex lens see prostitution as just another service industry. This comparison has become the basis of a perennial standard line of defense for the last several decades. "Professors, factory workers, lawyers, opera singers, prostitutes, doctors, legislators—we all do things with parts of our bodies, for which we receive a wage in return."[3] Because human beings are embodied beings, they cannot labor apart from using their bodies, even if they are doing "intellectual work." Some service providers, such as doctors, nurses and hospital orderlies, have very intimate contact with their clients. To some of those who see sex as just physical activity and physiological response, there seems to be nothing more problematic about selling sex than selling any other service or expertise. Such advocates of legitimating prostitution are not talking about situations in which young girls and boys are sold or kidnapped and made part of sex trafficking, whether domestic of international. Rather, they maintain that unless the particular prostitute is a "sexual slave" or is robbed (by severe economic or social disadvantages) of real alternatives to prostitution, selling sex for money seems consensual. So if prostitution is the sort of work some adult women and men choose to do, there is no ethical reason why they should not be able to enter into contractual relationships with willing buyers.

Such plain sex defenders of prostitution see attaching any stigma to "sex work" as irrational prejudice. Sex is not dirty or low. Some people have significant sexual skill. Why should they be restricted from selling their talents? Athletes, singers and professional dancers make a living off of physical talents that they enjoy exercising. Prostitutes should be able to do so as well. Some liberal feminists have seen discrimination against prostitution as discrimination against women, since the majority of prostitutes are female.

Plain sex supporters of prostitution often use consequence-based ethics in marshaling their arguments. Prostitution can be a chosen line of work, and prohibiting people from their chosen line of work causes more pain than pleasure. Clients of prostitutes also receive significant benefits from this work. Much of the pain connected with prostitution as it is now practiced is caused by social

stigma and the riskiness of a "profession" that has to be clandes-
tine because it is legally prohibited. The best ethical solution,
then, is to legalize prostitution and remove the stigma through
educating the general public.

Sometimes plain sex proponents use duty-oriented arguments
as well. Society at large, so these arguments go, has a duty to let
consenting adults do what they want for a living and form the
contractual agreements that they desire, unless there are serious
moral reasons that dictate otherwise. So society at large has a duty
to refrain from restricting the freedom of adult prostitutes and
their clients.

As we shall see when we look at prostitution through the expressive and power lenses, there are good reasons to think that
these defenses of prostitution are simplistic and unsatisfactory.
However, we should also acknowledge that those who are tempted
to defend prostitution are often well-intentioned. Too often in the
past, critics of prostitution have blamed only the prostitute and
not the client. Too often prostitutes were arrested far more frequently than their customers. Moreover, prostitutes often enter
prostitution out of pasts marred by abuse and economic disadvan-
tage. Those who have argued for the moral legitimacy of prostitution have often done so as a step in an argument toward its decriminalization. And one of the advantages noted about decriminalizing
prostitution is that once prostitution isn't a crime, it can be made
a safer line of work. We will be in a better position to comment on
this argument after examining the expressivist critique of prostitution, but first we will turn to how the plain sex lens sees the
production and consumption of pornography.

The Plain Sex Lens and Pornography

Many people who would never consider becoming a prostitute or
paying for the services of a prostitute are consumers of pornography. Internet pornography, adult cable channels, phone sex

and other forms of commercialized "virtual sex" have made the "old-fashioned" XXX video parlor largely obsolete. Ease of access has not only made the pornography industry a billion-dollar business but it has also pushed more than a few people from sexual continence toward sexual incontinence as consumers of pornographic material.[4]

Acting in a pornographic movie and providing phone sex are, like prostitution, types of "sex work." Those with a plain sex view argue that if pornography can be a significant source of pleasure for people, this is a harmless—perhaps even healthy—matter, since pleasure is itself a good. The pornography that they are defending is not, they will emphasize, violent or sadomasochistic. The kind of pornography they want to defend depicts consensual sex and is produced using actors who are willing participants.[5] Pornography that involves unwilling participants or depicts people being raped or degraded (even if these are simulated) will be morally problematic. But not all pornography is violent.

From the plain sex standpoint, it is unclear whether consequence-oriented ethical critiques of pornography are possible. Some have tried to draw causal connections between viewing pornography and sexual assault. We saw that some liberal feminists have marshaled a moral defense of sex work. But this is one of the large divides within feminism. Feminist philosopher Catherine MacKinnon advances a consequence-oriented argument against pornography. She argues that even nonviolent pornography makes habitual viewers statistically more likely to commit sexual assault than those who do not view pornography.[6] This empirical claim has been supported by some studies, but it has failed to be confirmed by other studies. And some have cited anecdotal evidence that pornography doesn't in fact incite sexual aggression. Now that pornography has become the "wallpaper" of so many people's lives, this has not turned men into "raving beasts" but has instead lessened male interest in real women.[7] Arguments that connect pornography with real-life sexual aggression appear flimsy to defenders of pornography. Later in this chapter we will see that for expressivists, more cogent consequence-oriented arguments against pornography are available.

THE EXPRESSIVE AND POWER LENSES AND PROSTITUTION

Through the plain sex lens both prostitution and pornography appear, for the most part, to be morally unproblematic practices. But the arguments that they have offered for their views seem simplistic to other thinkers, including many feminists. Carole Pateman is one of many feminist philosophers who maintain that prostitution is not only morally problematic but in fact damages *all* women. She claims that prostitution is the "public recognition of men as sexual masters; it puts submission on sale as a commodity on the market."[8] This affects not just the women who sell sex but all other women, because the practice makes women into commodities. Feminists like Pateman have many concerns about prostitution. Many of the women and girls involved are in fact operating with little real choice. Many come from abusive situations and see themselves as "good for nothing" else. Many see their only worth as being an attractive body. Many see no real financial or cultural alternative to sex work. Prostitution exploits women who have already been abused and injured by patriarchy.

Notice that Pateman is looking at sexuality through both a power lens and an expressive lens. She thinks that the sex sold by a prostitute and bought by her client is not plain sex, but sexuality freighted with imaginative and symbolic significance about male power over women. Testimonies from particular former prostitutes corroborate Pateman's analysis. Naomi Wolf quotes a former sex worker responding to movies like *Pretty Woman*: "Here is all I have to say about how they are glamorizing those images for girls. . . . When men think a woman is a whore, it's open . . . season . . .

on her. They can be absolutely as crass and vile and violent and cruel and uncaring as the darkest part of their personality wants to be. And it's okay. They don't have to afford the woman *one ounce* of respect for being a human being. She's not a human being. She's a thing."[9]

Those holding plain sex views have offered rebuttals to these expressivist objections to prostitution. These rebuttals claim that male subjugation of women is not a characteristic of prostitution per se but that it is at most a characteristic of how prostitution is most often enacted in our society. What is objectionable, it is claimed, is not the sale of sex but the subjugation of women. The two can be separated, at least in principle. Prostitution could conceivably take place between sex workers and clients who meet in conditions of equality, rather than subjugation.

But Yolanda Estes, a former prostitute who is now an academic philosopher, thinks that prostitution is morally problematic precisely because what it sells is plain sex. She reflects on the psychic bifurcation that is a necessary element in the relationship of prostitute and client. Estes states, "The prostitute attempts to annihilate her presence within the sexual act by extinguishing her reactions to it. Mindful of the risk posed by intense feelings that are otherwise likely to occur, she estranges herself from her body, presenting a phantom of the sensibility that she forbids herself to possess. When the illusion dissolves she is expected to reintegrate her alienated self with her prostituted flesh."[10] Sex *should* be about giving way to one's desires and subjective experiences. But prostitutes cannot let their guard down; they know that their job is to please their client, no matter how they may be experiencing what is happening. Whether she is disgusted, bored or fearful, the prostitute must feign arousal.

Estes's ethical evaluation of prostitution is based on duty-oriented ethics. She concludes that prostitution is immoral because it violates our duty to respect humanity in ourselves and others. The psychic bifurcation required in making sex a commodity dehumanizes both the prostitute and the client. Alienation from one's own embodied self is not what sex *should* express.

Philosopher S. E. Marshall agrees with Estes that sex as plain sex is itself morally objectionable—at least if the sex is so plain as to leave open the question of whether there is any degree of mutuality in the sexual exchange. Marshall asks how far the analogy between sex work and nursing or waiting tables can be pushed. She thinks the answer is "Not very far." Could we picture prostitution being on a list of options in a career counseling office or in a retraining center for the unemployed? Could we envision a certification program for prostitutes and a customer bill of rights for johns?

Applying ideas borrowed from philosopher Martha Nussbaum, Marshall argues that sexual behaviors that objectify people are morally problematic. Two types of objectification are relevant. The first type treats people as nonsubjects, as "something whose experience and feelings (if any) need not be taken into account." The second type of objectification treats people as interchangeable with others in the way *things* are interchangeable. The technical term for this second type of objectification is treating someone as "fungible."[11]

Marshall argues that the commercialization of sex makes the sex worker into a fungible provider of a fungible commodity. Moreover, the person purchasing sexual services from another is paying for the "right" to use them as a sexual object without regard to the sex worker's subjectivity. Though some prostitutes simulate pleasure in order to facilitate "customer satisfaction" and others may be aroused by their work (at least some of the time), their clients do not see concern about the pleasure of the prostitute as obligatory or even appropriate. After all, the prostitute is being paid!

Marshall acknowledges that within some commercial contexts it is morally acceptable to treat one person as interchangeable with another. Routinely, any sales clerk will do when making a purchase; any waiter will do when ordering dinner. Fungibility is not, then, in and of itself, sufficient to make an interaction morally wrong. Marshall observes:

> To treat people as interchangeable within . . . market activity need not be in any way damaging. Indeed, it is perfectly possible to imagine that with developments in robotics we could do without waiters altogether without loss. In this way they might seem to be fungible. . . . One reason why fungibility of waiters is not damaging is that the job performed by the waiter does not engage anything significant to their personhood. No aspect of them as a person is seriously trammeled.[12]

But our sexuality, unlike our ability to record a person's choice from a menu and bring food to their table, is "an aspect of our selves as social creatures, it is one of the ways in which we engage with other people seen from a personal perspective."[13]

Sex, if it is to be something more valuable than sex with a sex toy, is a way of engaging social persons. Sex needs to acknowledge the partner's subjectivity, or it objectifies in a way that denies humanity. If we recognize humanity in sexual encounters, there must be some degree of mutuality. Robots are fungible; if one breaks down, we can replace it with a replica. Robots also lack subjectivity. But human beings are subjects, not fungibles. Because sexuality is social, robotic sex partners (even really "hot" ones) cannot give us what humans seek in sexual activity. People who would find sex with a robot attractive would be seen as having a fetish, not as participating in a valuable human activity. Marshall concludes that sex must involve an essential aspect of acknowledged subjectivity on the part of the participants if it is to be intelligibly valued as a human activity. This means that sexual partners cannot be fungible in the way that waiters are fungible, without denying the humanity of the partner. The commercialization of sexual activity is thus dehumanizing and morally objectionable, even if it could be practiced in a way that was not sexist or patriarchal.

Sex that is salable has become less than *human* sex. Sex so plain as to be robbed of the mutuality inherent in human sexuality dehumanizes the participants. Purchased sex is unworthy of both the seller and the buyer. These important insights help us understand why prostitution dehumanizes sex for both the customer and the sex worker.

We can now see that the plain sex defenses of prostitution, though well intentioned, are confused. Prostitution is not a morally acceptable practice. Yet defenders of prostitution have highlighted fragments of truth that should not be discarded. Sex workers *are* often motivated by desperation. If we think that this is a line of work that no woman or man should choose, we should also care about addressing the underlying problems. Christians as well as principled secularists should seek to diminish the abuse, neglect, poverty and addiction that are the back story for many prostitutes having gone into sex work in the first place.

THE EXPRESSIVE AND POWER LENSES AND PORNOGRAPHY

Those with expressive and power lenses have many of the same objections to pornography as they do to prostitution. Feminist legal scholar Catharine A. MacKinnon disputes the claim that sex is ever just about uninterpreted and unalloyed physical pleasure. "There is no irreducible essence, no 'just sex,'" MacKinnon emphatically asserts.[14] Sex is never plain sex. MacKinnon supports this claim by an appeal to pervasiveness of both sexuality and enculturation. We are taught how to be sexual by both overt and subtle cultural messages. Sexuality is pervasive rather than a discrete area of human life.

Sex always expresses something, and what it expresses in pornography is the subordination of women. "Dominance eroticized defines the imperatives of masculinity, submission eroticized defines femininity. So many of the distinctive features of women's status as second class—the restriction and constraint and contortion, the servility and the display, the self-mutilation and requisite presentation of self as a beautiful thing, the enforced passivity, the humiliation—are made into the content of sex for women."[15] Pornography doesn't just mirror this inequality—it is an active agent in the creation of the subordination of women. MacKinnon claims that "what pornography *does* goes beyond its content: it eroticizes hierarchy; it sexualizes inequality. It makes dominance and submission into sex."[16]

Although Yolanda Estes does not extend the application of her points about prostitution to pornography, the bifurcation of consciousness that she describes in prostitution seems to apply equally to those who act in pornographic videos. Whether their arousal is genuine or simulated, these actors surely must be experiencing some of the same self-monitoring and distancing from their sexual response that Estes describes among prostitutes. So the production of pornography is morally problematic from an expressive point of view. And if it is immoral to produce pornography, it is immoral to consume pornography, for doing so contributes to sustaining it and is participating in an immoral practice.

Philosopher Harry Brod presents a striking expressivist argument about the effect of pornography on the male consumer. He observes that in pornography men are routinely depicted as "sexual acrobats endowed with oversized and overused organs."[17] Women in pornography are depicted as perpetually available and eager for sex. Brod goes on to reflect that men whose expectations are tutored by pornography often find that women do not meet these expectations. Real women are far more complicated than the eager women depicted in pornography. Men tutored by pornography find women deficient to the extent that the women fall short

of the expectations created by pornography. Men may try to remedy their disappointment by fantasying about pornographic images during sex rather than focusing on their real-life partner.
Pornography also contributes to male performance anxiety, which
creates its own version of bifurcated consciousness. "Relating to
one's body as a performance machine produces a split consciousness wherein part of one's attention is watching the machine,
looking for flaws in its performance, even while one is supposedly
immersed in the midst of sensual pleasure. This produces a self-
distancing self-consciousness which mechanizes sex and reduces
pleasure."[18]

Notice that Brod's points about the effect of pornography on
what is "in the head" of consumers provide fuel for objections
using both duty-oriented and consequence-oriented approaches
to sexual ethics. From the perspective of duty, one who allows his
or her sexual consciousness to be shaped by pornography may be
falling short in both duties to himself or herself, as well as duties
to his or her sexual partner. Being fully present within one's sexuality during sex is an important aspect of being human. To undermine this capacity in one's self fails to respect one's own humanity. One also has a duty to one's sexual partner to be fully present
to him or her during sexual intercourse. To have undermined
one's capacity to be fully present is disrespectful to one's partner.

From the perspective of consequence-oriented ethics, the consumer of pornography is risking trading short-term, lower-grade
pleasures for longer-term, higher-quality pleasure. The "mecha-
nized sex" that is the side effect of a sexual consciousness shaped
by pornography is substandard compared to fully present sex.
Arousal while viewing pornography does produce pleasure, but
this may not compensate for the amount of pleasure lost through
the "distancing self-consciousness" that Brod notes as an effect of
pornography. He also thinks that this distancing is very likely to
have bad consequences for one's partner—that those whose con-

sciousness is shaped by pornography are likely to be less attentive and, to the degree that they are "distanced," inferior lovers.

Harry Brod is not the only philosopher to make such observations. Joan Mason-Grant emphasizes that the consumption of pornography is itself a sexual practice. Pornography enlists its consumers to engage, over and over, in having "sex with another without actually having to directly interact with, or be accountable to, the sexual other."[19] Pornography teaches its consumers that their own arousal is what matters. Pornography teaches them to expect that women want to be mere objects of someone else's arousal. Consequently, the use of pornography is rehearsal for sexual narcissism. What we rehearse over and over affects who we become.[20] What we risk becoming through the routine consumption of pornography is a less than fully human sexual being.

These arguments from Brod and Mason-Grant diagnose dynamics that are intimately connected to the nature of pornographic viewing. Their objections go deep and are more powerful than the traditional consequence-oriented critiques of pornography that we examined earlier. While the empirical evidence for the link between viewing pornography and sexual assault is arguably ambiguous, claims about whether pornography leads to self-conscious distancing and sexual selfishness are issues that can be settled by self-reflection on the part of those who routinely use pornography. Users who are honestly asking themselves whether they should continue can weigh whether what Brod and Mason-Grant say rings true in their own experience.

PORNOGRAPHY VERSUS EROTICA

Before leaving the subject of pornography, we should consider the distinction that expressivists often draw between pornography and erotica. Many expressivists think that this distinction makes a moral difference—that although pornography is morally problematic, erotica is not. One way of making the distinction is that

erotica depicts mutuality within a sexual encounter, while pornography shows one character objectifying another character.
Another way of drawing the distinction is that erotica depicts
sexual encounters between *persons*—humans who are more than
the sum of their sexualized body parts—while pornography depicts bodies that have been reduced to sexualized body parts.
Expressivists emphasize the importance of the imaginative significance of sex. Those who champion erotica see the imaginative
significance of erotica as unproblematic, even positive. In contrast, they see the imaginative significance of pornography as
very problematic indeed.

We haven't said much in this chapter about the romantic view,
because romanticists have had little to say on the subjects of pornography and prostitution. But those who see sex through the romantic lens might, like the expressivists, see some types of erotica
as morally acceptable. Romantics might think that the best and
most appropriate kind of erotica depicts erotic encounters between
characters who are in love with one another. Many romance novels have one or more erotic scenes in them. And many who would
not dream of accessing pornography see nothing wrong with enjoying one of these romance novels, no matter how "steamy" its
lovemaking scenes might be.

Is this distinction between pornography and erotica convinc-
ing and helpful? Harry Brod thinks it is. This is because he focuses on how the *content* of the material tutors the viewer's or
reader's sensibility. The content of erotica depicts sexual encounters as something that approximates what human sexuality *should*
express. So Brod sees reading or viewing erotica as a good thing.
But Joan Mason-Grant emphasizes what the viewer or reader of
the material is *practicing*. Are they viewing or reading erotica in
order to become aroused? If so, they are still engaging in the practice of seeking arousal without directly interacting with another
human being. In such cases, erotica still habituates sexual narcis-

sism. This is not an assertion Mason-Grant makes herself, because she does not specifically discuss erotica. However, this application and conclusion seem to be natural extensions of her view. If what I am seeking in erotica is a simulacrum of a sexual encounter, then this might be somewhat better than seeking arousal through pornography. But how much better? Setting out to become aroused by reading about or viewing depictions of fully human sexual mutuality is still an isolated, narcissistic experience—a less than fully human expression of my sexuality. To the extent that erotica actually succeeds in its goal—depicting "sexual subjects, manifesting their personhood in and through their bodies,"[21] our reaction to finding ourselves aroused should be one of embarrassment—as if we'd stumbled on our friends in the throes of lovemaking. Would we subject them to a voyeuristic gaze? So the relevant moral question about erotica seems to be: What am I after? What am I letting myself practice?

PROSTITUTION, PORNOGRAPHY AND THE COVENANTAL LENS

So what lessons can those of us with a covenantal lens as our central focus learn from all of this? First, perceptive readers may have noted that the expressivist critiques of prostitution and pornography share considerable common ground with the criticism of casual sex that we encountered in chapter six. Those who engage in casual sex treat their partners as replaceable collections of body parts. Those who buy and sell sex disrespect the humanity of themselves and others by treating sexuality as something that can be disassociated from personhood. Those who act in or consume pornography do likewise. Proponents of the plain sex view are consistent in dismissing all of these claims as prudish or utopian. I think that such people are wrong, but they are at least being consistent.

What is more puzzling are those who claim to see the world

through a covenantal or even a romantic lens but who try to make moral distinctions among casual sex, the consumption of pornography, and buying or selling sex. Even from an expressivist perspective, all of these practices are morally problematic for very similar reasons. From the perspective of a covenantal or romantic view, both of which are supposed to have more stringent standards for sexual involvement than the expressive view, what good reason would there be to criminalize prostitution but treat casual sex and the consumption of pornography as private personal choices?[22]

What about the questions that we started with at the beginning of this chapter? Should Christians shop at Victoria's Secret or take Viagra? How can we distinguish between the exploitive objectification of the human body and the admirable expressiveness of the nude in art? What this debate between expressivists and plain sex proponents has shown us is that in areas where "Just say no" is too simple a response, the appropriate response is to ask: What are we practicing? What are we habituating ourselves to feel? What ways of seeing others are we making second nature to us?

As we saw in chapter three, from a covenantal perspective the answer to these questions should be chastity; sexual integrity should be our aspiration. Why are you taking Viagra? In order to continue to be a good lover to your wife? Or out of desperation rooted in seeing your whole personhood wrapped up in potency? Answers here will make a difference in whether chastity is or is not at issue. Similar things can be said about whether one is shopping for sexy underwear at Victoria's Secret in order to feel "porn worthy," or whether in contemplating a nude one is treating it as a titillating collection of body parts.

Chastity cannot be cultivated apart from self-knowledge. Sexual integrity is also supported by an array of other virtues that we will discuss in the conclusion.

CONCLUSION

TOWARD SEXUAL INTEGRITY

In high school and early college I had a recurring anxiety dream. I was on a lush lawn and one of my contact lenses had dropped into the grass. This would have presented a considerable challenge in the relatively sane and predictable world of waking life. But the world of my dreams had its own logic—a logic whose goal was making the difficult impossible. In my dreams the lawn was always rife with contact lenses—some were a size similar to my own; some the size of dinner plates; some four feet in diameter. None of them were mine. The dream ended with my pulse racing, panic jarring me awake with fear of never being able to find my own lens.

At the time, I took these dreams to be prosaic—mapping a waking fear with ham-handed literalism into my sleep. I didn't want to replace a lost contact lens. Having dropped a lens from time to time, I'd spent more time than I wanted on hands and knees brushing gently with my hands over the floor, hoping to scare up a lost lens without scratching it, worrying the whole time I'd crush it under a knee.

But looking back at my dreamscape, I'm sure that my psyche was playing with a double entendre to grapple with more important fears. I *was* anxious about losing a contact lens, but I was even more anxious about losing my perspective among all of the alternative points of view I was being exposed to in my college studies. My dreams were posing important questions: How was I to process the many different views I was encountering? Had I permanently lost my perspective? Would the world forever be a scary place that I would only half see? Would an enlarged world of multiple perspectives contribute to more maturity and heightened clarity or lead to permanent myopia?

These sorts of anxieties make some Christians reticent or defensive about engaging in dialogue about the cultural alternatives that surround them. Caution is not unwarranted. There *are* attractive yet distorted perspectives. Changing our viewpoint doesn't always increase truthful or clear vision. But a refusal to engage with alternative perspectives has its own grave risks. Sometimes the way that we have always seen things is in need of correction, clarification, expansion. How will we know whether this is so unless we are willing to reflect and reconsider? And if we are unwilling to at least try to see how the world looks through other lenses, we are unlikely to be able to make our own perspective understandable to those with alternative views. Why should people who differ from us give us a hearing if we are unwilling to treat their perspectives with respect?

This essay has attempted to increase understanding of the perspectives on sexuality that are prevalent in our culture, whether they are Christian or secular. We have seen that these perspectives have strengths and limitations. We should acknowledge the strengths of each of the six perspectives we have considered with gratitude for the insights they yield.

In examining the plain sex view we have seen that it has an internal logic and standards for sexual behavior. Because consent is so crucial to how those with a plain sex view distinguish acceptable from unacceptable behavior, proponents of this view have done us all a service in showing how complex the issues surrounding valid sexual consent are. The plain sex view's focus on pleasure has also motivated research and education that has helped many attain more satisfying sex lives than they would have if left with less knowledge.

The power perspective teaches us to employ what philosophers call the "hermeneutics of suspicion," critically examining the power dynamics that are at work as we and others deploy our sexuality. "Who really benefits?" and "Where are the payoffs?" are the questions the power perspective urges us to ask.

The expressive perspective on sexuality has helped us all to learn to ask important questions about sexual attitudes and comportment: "What am I after?" "What am I communicating?" "What am I practicing?"

The romantic perspective reveals how fitting sexual intercourse is as a consummation of loving desire. "I long for us to be one" is aptly expressed sexually.

The procreative view increases our awareness of how our "contraceptive culture" often robs sex of the awe and reverence owed this central aspect of our humanity. Sex links ancestors with posterity; it's more than a private arena of personal preference.

The covenantal perspective emphasizes that solemn promises before God and others create the most fitting context for full sexual expression.

We have also seen that, taken in isolation, each of these perspectives is fragmentary and potentially distortive. Writer and social critic Wendell Berry observes that the plain sex view, at its plainest, "is and can only be a dispirited description of the working of a sort of anatomical machinery . . . a sexuality that is neither erotic nor social nor sacramental but rather a cold-blooded, abstract procedure that is finally not even imaginable."[1] What the plain sex lens cannot see is that sex that is only about bodies is less than fully human.

The expressive lens sees that sex is not just about bodies but is also "in the head." Yet, in itself, it cannot tell us enough about what we should be expressing and with whom we should be using "body language."

Seen only through the power lens, sex is doomed to forever be the arena in which we seek to objectify others before they objectify us.

The romantic lens too often holds us hostage to our fantasies of a perfect lover, sending us into either a frenetic search for techniques to fan the flames of passion or, failing that, into serial monogamy as romantic passion fades.

Stereotypes of the procreative view that reduce it to the proper use of genitalia and fecundity are exaggerations; yet its strictures on reasonable uses of contraception for family planning do put the unitive aspects of marital sexuality at risk in real life. And both the procreative and the covenantal view have tempted some sexual ethicists who hold them to spend inordinate time proctoring the perimeters of marriage while neglecting the quality of marital sexuality itself.

If we take these lenses as isolated and we are faced with the choice posed by my dreams—which lens should we take up as our own?—we are left in a quandary. But the metaphor of the phoropter shifts our question: How can we combine these lenses in a way that avoids heterophoria and promotes orthophoria? To the extent that we suffer from heterophoria, we have blurred vision resulting from a faulty combination of lenses—multiplicity without convergence. We surrender to relativism or a "choose your own adventure" mentality about sexual conduct. Orthophoria is the happy outcome when multiplicity plus convergence yields depth perception and clarity. The world is in focus—we have 20/20 vision.

The thesis of this essay has been that orthophoria regarding sexuality—optimal sexual insight—occurs when the covenantal lens is the central focus while aided by the procreative, power, expressive, romantic and plain sex lenses in their proper relation to it. Sexual insight aids and is aided by the development of chastity—the successful integration of sexuality that results in inner unity between bodily and spiritual being. Chastity is the key sexual virtue. Thus this essay's prevailing emphasis has been a virtue-oriented approach to sexual ethics.

Chastity is not grim resolve but, when fully developed, a joyful and highly useful virtue. Chastity allows us to take our sexuality with us wherever we go without treating other people as collections of sexualized body parts. If we are married, chastity allows us to desire our husband or wife as a whole person—body and soul. Chastity allows us to make love in a way that celebrates our wife's or husband's whole embodied self, extended from remembered times and to anticipated times. Chastity helps us be faithful to our husband or wife in health, in sickness and ultimately in death. If we are single, chastity allows us to be sexual while refraining from intercourse and without being restless. Whether married or single, chastity allows us to be happily and robustly embodied—to be content, yet aware and appreciative of our own body and the bodies of others.

Chastity is an ideal. Some people in reading a paragraph like the one you just read would be angry at what sounds unrealistic or hypocritical to them. No one is her or his best self all the time. But this is to misunderstand the nature of ideals. In her essay "An Expedition to the Pole," writer Annie Dillard compares our journey toward intimacy with God to the nineteenth-century expeditions that made attempt after attempt to reach the North Pole. The quest for the Pole was arduous. Those who were finally successful had to learn to know themselves and to adapt to polar conditions. Dillard wryly observes that "wherever we go, there seems to be only one business at hand—that of finding workable compromises between the sublimity of our ideas and the absurdity of the fact of us."[2] This observation applies to polar exploration, to our spiritual life, and to grappling with and attending to our sexuality. An ideal is, to use Dillard's phrases, both a "Pole of the Most Trouble" and a "pole of great price." An ideal is a lofty aspiration that sets in motion a moral quest.

Used foolishly, ideals oppress people. We can use them to flail ourselves and bludgeon others. But used wisely, ideals can keep us moving in the right direction. They can serve as compass points in charting the course of our lives. Chastity would be a useful virtue whether any particular one of us ever perfectly exemplified it. By aiming at chastity, some of us will at most attain continence. But if we lower our aspirations and aim only at continence, we are more likely to lapse into incontinence. And to the extent that we excuse our incontinence as being "only human," we are likely to slide into vice. Taking chastity seriously as an *ideal* can help us admit when we are nowhere near there yet while resolving to become better. We can be more truthful with ourselves about ourselves. And we can be duly grateful and admiring when we become or meet those who have reached the goal of chastity itself.

Annie Dillard notes that there is no such thing as a solo polar explorer. As bumbling as communities are, we need communities to survive and thrive—especially if we are on a moral quest. American Christianity in the twenty-first century too often treats the Christian life as a solo endeavor. Nowhere is this more true than in our quest for sexual integrity. If more Christians took chastity seriously as an ideal—an ideal genuinely sought but which few have fully reached—this could open up a space for real conversation within the church about our struggles and growing edges. Less energy would be wasted on a pretense of propriety. Too often in the church, sexuality is treated with polite silence, hushed confessions, titillated gossip or diatribes. Mutual support is impossible under such conditions. Acknowledging chastity as an ideal and making sexual integrity our corporate quest can give us the courage to be frank and the grace to be compassionate.

There are no solo polar explorers. There are also no stand-alone virtues. Virtues are like the fingers on a hand—not all the same size, having different functions, but growing proportionally as the hand grows. Virtues are like the poles of a teepee or stones in an arch. Rightly related, the virtues are mutually supporting.

A quest for chastity or sexual integrity is supported, enabled and sustained by virtues that have wider application than sexuality. Chastity is an instance of moderation or temperance—the ability to live graciously with our appetites for food, alcohol, stimulants, rest and possessions. Moderation helps us act on our knowledge of the distinction between healthily satisfying our desires and enslavement. Important examples of other virtues that support chastity are justice, mutual respect, compassion and consideration. Too often people who see these as important virtues for other aspects of life leave them behind when they enter the dating scene or cross the threshold of their own homes. People who understand these virtues know that "All's fair in love and war" is a dangerous lie.

The virtues of justice and mutual respect link a virtue-oriented approach to ethics with a duty-oriented approach. Those who are careful to fulfill their duties act justly, but justice is not a mere matter of following rules. Justice as a virtue helps us recognize when rights are at stake and rules are applicable. The just person refrains from stealing and goes beyond that. The just person returns the money when they've been given too much change. The just person takes up their fair share of burdensome tasks that need doing but are no one's particular duty.

Justice, when exercised with regard to our sexuality, helps us do more than avoid adultery and date rape. Justice helps us recognize when flirtation has escalated to seduction and when "consent" has been secured by manipulation or wheedling. Mutual respect helps us recognize that what goes on sexually between consenting adults can at times be mutually exploitive. Two people exercising mutual respect will refrain from becoming "friends with benefits" because they realize that providing each other with a convenient means for satisfying sexual hunger cheapens them both. "Friendship with benefits" is not friendship *plus,* but rather a friendship that has fallen short of the respect that friends owe one another and their friendship.

The virtues of compassion and consideration link a virtue-oriented approach to ethics with the consequence-oriented approach. Whether our actions cause more pleasure than pain for those affected by what we do is an important ethical concern. But compassion and consideration do more than apply a "hedonistic calculus" and act on the resulting calculations. Compassion helps us vividly imagine how our actions will affect others and how we would feel if we were in their shoes. Compassion helps us avoid suffering before it happens and tries to remedy it when it occurs.

Compassion, when exercised with regard to our sexuality, prevents us from acting as if enticing the sexual desires of others when they cannot ethically be satisfied is "just having a good time." Consideration reminds us that our quest for sexual integrity is a corporate matter and that how we dress and who and how we touch can hinder others in their quest. Compassion inures us from enjoying pornography by helping us see that the actors are themselves real human beings who are someone's daughter or son. Could we enjoy viewing pornography populated by our closest friends? Could we buy sex from someone if we thought vividly about the sex worker's childhood or their present family lives? Or how they estrange themselves from their bodies while dealing with their clients? Compassion bolsters fidelity in marriage by making the pain that we might cause our spouse a potent antidote to wandering attractions. Consideration between spouses helps them attune their sexual desires and rhythms. Compassion and consideration can also bolster resolve about abstinence in single-ness if, before embarking on an affair or hookup, we imagine viv-idly what the dissolution of a temporary bond will cost not just us, but the other.

Justice and compassion are also important to responding ap-propriately to sexual incontinence or vice in others. Compassion for frail human beings struggling unsuccessfully to achieve con-tinence can keep us from being self-righteous or judgmental if it is our responsibility to address instances of sexual misconduct. But compassion and justice for those whose rights are violated or who suffer harm caused by the sexual lapses of others also keeps our compassion for perpetrators from becoming complicit with repeat offense.

There are still other virtues that can aid us in our quest for sexual integrity. Some of these are more lighthearted than justice and compassion. Creativity and playfulness can help married cou-ples find continuing sexual satisfaction within their marriage without lapsing into the mutual disrespect of demanding that one's spouse be "porn worthy." Gratitude for the privilege of hav-ing one's total gift of self honored and reciprocated can make vio-lating that gift unthinkable. Reverence is a less lighthearted virtue than playfulness and creativity, but it is no less fitting a response than gratitude to the experience of being naked and unafraid, day upon day, year upon year, with one's spouse. Sexual intercourse is an arena for a particularly valuable combination of full engage-ment, self-abandonment and attunement with one's beloved. The covenantal view, when taken as a central organizing lens of the other five sexual lenses, is designed to tutor us in the virtues that make approximating this ideal a real possibility.

The covenantal view, when taken as the central organizing lens, also provides a sexual ideal for those who are unmarried. To be sure, chastity in singleness is very different from chastity in mar-riage. Others than I are better positioned to discuss the specific application of general virtues and chastity to singleness. I've been married too much of my adult life to have any wisdom gained from experience on such matters. From the outside looking in, it appears that unmarried people who best approximate chastity are those who find arenas other than the bedroom for exercising creativity, playfulness and gratitude. Such people cultivate deep friendships. They find ways of being physically expressive without being genital. As someone who has been married most of my adult life, I have great respect for those who are able to go beyond continence in singleness and cultivate chastity, especially in cases where singleness is not a voluntary choice. Those whose circumstances and commitment to the covenantal view lead them to treat chastity in singleness as a "Pole of the Most Trouble" deserve more than our respect. They deserve whatever help we can provide through our companionship in our shared quest for sexual integrity.

Whatever our circumstances, wherever we are along the way, the quest for sexual integrity is a noble quest. We need, and should be for one another, a community of encouragement as we strive to be our best selves.

Those for whom chastity seems a distant goal often have a deep sense of loneliness—whether they are single, in a difficult marriage or simply find themselves with inordinate desires. Their loneliness is often exacerbated by a sense that continence demands missing out on a significant source of self-transcendence. Sex has become so relentlessly consuming in our society in no small part because, for many, orgasm is the *only* way they experience self-transcendence. Sex gives them not just pleasure and release, but the closest approximation they have to an encounter with the mystical. With the decline of significant roles for religion and the arts in our culture, sexual ecstasy fills the hole vacated by the sublime.

Sex *can* be a source of self-transcendence but it is far from the most important source. Those struggling with incontinence may have a problem larger than unruly appetites. Some may be motivated by what C. S. Lewis called joy or *Sehnsucht* (German for "longing") but have misidentified its nature and source. *Sehnsucht* is the ache we get when even the best we have encountered falls short of what we long for. Lewis translates *Sehnsucht* as "joy" because this ache, once experienced, leaves us wanting the ache again and again. It is "an unsatisfied desire which is itself more desirable than any other satisfaction."[3] Though an ache, joy is the highest pleasure of which humans are capable. *Sehnsucht* is longing for the transcendent—a longing ultimately fulfilled by God alone. All the best sex we could possibly fit into a human life would still leave us with unsatisfied longing—unless it deadened us to genuine joy.

But our society tells us otherwise. If we could just find the perfect lover, we could live happily ever after, so the story goes. Christianity tells an alternative story—or rather, the same story, but with a startling twist. God is our only perfect lover. "Seek greater intimacy with God" may sound hollow to those struggling with sexual loneliness—like saying "Let them eat cake" to those without bread. But all of us, married or single, happy or restless, need to keep these two truths in mind: our sexuality is a very good, albeit difficult, gift; and sex is not our savior.

NOTES

Introduction

[1]Beth Ann Fennelly, "From L'Hotel Terminus Notebooks," in *Open House* (New York: W. W. Norton, 2009), p. 52.

[2]For fuller discussion of this topic see my article "Judgmentalism," *Faith and Philosophy* 6, no. 3 (July 1989): 275-87.

[3]Donna Freitas, *Sex and the Soul: Juggling Sexuality, Spirituality, Romance and Religion on America's College Campuses* (New York: Oxford University Press, 2008), p. 135.

[4]Ibid., p. 168.

Chapter 1: Six Sexual Lenses

[1]John S. Grabowski, *Sex and Virtue: An Introduction to Sexual Ethics* (Washington, D.C.: Catholic University of America Press, 2003), p. 86. There are a host of subtle and not so subtle differences in views of sexuality influenced by religions other than Christianity. Up to the present, they have had less influence on U.S. culture than Christianity has—a situation that may change as multiculturalism escalates. For a useful survey of views of sexuality from a crosscultural perspective see Margret A. Farley, "Diverse Crossings," in *Just Love: A Framework for Christian Sexual Ethics* (New York: Continuum, 2008), pp. 57-108.

[2]Denis de Rougemont's *Love in the Western World,* trans. Montgomery Belgion (New York: Harcourt, Brace, 1940) sets out what has become the predominate story of the development of the romantic conception of love. De Rougemont attributes major aspects of this development to the troubadours' ballads of the late medieval period.

[3]Richard Taylor, *Having Love Affairs* (Buffalo: Prometheus, 1982), p. 12.

[4]Mike W. Martin, *Love's Virtues* (Lawrence: University Press of Kansas, 1996), p. 82.

[5]Alan Goldman, "Plain Sex," *Philosophy and Public Affairs* 6 (1977): 267-87.

[6]Igor Primoratz, *Ethics and Sex* (New York: Routedge, 1999), pp. 32-33.

[7]To take just one example, a *New York Magazine* article on online personal ads asserted that New Yorkers using the Internet to find sex "aren't people who necessarily have trouble getting laid—they just want to get laid more." Vanessa Grigoriadis, "The New Position on Casual Sex," accessed January 6, 2003, http://nymag.com/nymetro/news/features/n_8227/.

[8]Sallie Tisdale, *Talk Dirty to Me* (New York: Anchor, 1994), p. 16. Let the reader beware—some of Tisdale's ruminations concerning pornography border on pornographic.

[9]Carter Heyward, *Touching Our Strength: The Erotic as Power and the Love of God* (New York: Harper & Row, 1989), p. 27.

[10]Robert C. Solomon, "Sexual Paradigms," *Journal of Philosophy* 71, no. 11 (1974): 343-44.

[11]Jennie Yabroff, "The Myths of Teen Sexuality," *Newsweek*, June 9, 2008, p. 55.

[12]Aristotle *Nicomachean Ethics* 1.7.1145b4-10, trans. Terence Irwin, 2nd ed. (New York: Hackett, 2000).

Chapter 2: Marital Sexuality

[1]Gordon Graham, "Commitment and the Value of Marriage," in *Person to Person*, ed. Gordon Graham and Hugh Lafollette (Philadelphia: Temple University Press, 1989), p. 200.

[2]Lucia Perillo, *I've Heard the Vultures Singing: Field Notes on Poetry, Illness and Nature* (San Antonio: Trinity University Press, 2007), p. 135.

[3]Ibid., p. 143.

[4]Adam Phillips, *Monogamy* (New York: Pantheon, 1996).

[5]See, for example, Michel Foucault's *History of Sexuality* (New York: Vintage Books, 1990), for a detailed analysis of the many ways that power can be deployed in connection with sexuality.

[6]Jeffrey Weeks, *Invented Moralities: Sexual Values in an Age of Uncertainty* (New York: Columbia University Press, 1995), p. 174.

[7]C. S. Lewis, *The Four Loves* (New York: Harcourt Brace Jovanovich, 1960), p. 132.

[8]Alongside this idea that "good women" are not interested in sex, runs a parallel belief in women as wanton seductresses. This has been labeled the "Madonna/whore" syndrome and is widely studied by historians, sociologists, literary and artistic critics, and others.

[9]John Witte Jr., "Looking Back," in *Marriage: Just a Piece of Paper?* ed. Katherine Anderson, Don Browning and Brian Boyer (Grand Rapids: Eerdmans, 2002), pp. 238-39.

[10]See de Rougemont, *Love in the Western World.*

[11]Caroline J. Simon, *The Disciplined Heart: Love, Destiny, and Imagination* (Grand Rapids: Eerdmans, 1997). See especially chap. 5 (pp. 109-43).

[12]David Matzko McCarthy, *Sex and Love in the Home* (London: SCM Press, 2001), p. 8.

[13]Ibid., pp. 215-17.

[14]Richard B. Hays, *The Moral Vision of the New Testament: A Contemporary Introduction to New Testament Ethics* (San Francisco: HarperSanFrancisco, 1996), p. 372.

[15]John Shelby Spong, "Can the Church Bless Divorce?" *Christian Century,* November 28, 1984, pp. 1126-27.

[16]Susan Cheever, *Desire: Where Sex Meets Addiction* (New York: Simon and Schuster, 2008), pp. 65-66.

[17]Hays, *Moral Vision of the New Testament,* p. 372.

[18]Wendell Berry, *Sex, Economy, Freedom and Community* (New York: Pantheon, 1992), pp. 138-39.

[19]G. E. M. Anscombe, "Contraception and Chastity," *The Human World* 7 (1972): 18.

[20]Ibid. G. E. M. (Elizabeth) Anscombe was one of the most well-known English-speaking woman philosophers in the mid-twentieth century. She was a student of Ludwig Wittgenstein, whose philosophy had enormous influence. She helped ensure Wittgenstein's influence through her translation of his *Philosophical Investigations.* An important philosopher in her own right, Anscombe's article "Modern Moral Philosophy" was instrumental in reviving an interest in discussions of virtue among ethicists. This article, as well as her translation of Wittgenstein's *Philosophical Investigations,* is widely quoted and treated with respect. In contrast, her article "Contraception and Chastity" is little known and almost completely ignored within academic philosophical circles. Perhaps this is because of the starkness of her rendition of the procreative view of sexuality.

[21]Anscombe, "Contraception and Chastity," p. 23.

[22]Grabowski, *Sex and Virtue,* p. 81.

[23]Ibid., p. 131.

[24]This theological commitment also has some empirical support. Psychologist David G. Myers argues that there is empirical evidence that monogamy and marriage contribute significantly to happiness and well-being. He also presents evidence that premarital sexual activity detracts from the likeli-

hood of successful marriage. See his *The American Paradox* (New Haven, Conn.: Yale University Press, 2000).

Chapter 3: Virginity and Chastity

[1]Betty Becker-Theye, *The Seducer as Mythic Figure in Richardson, Laclos and Kierkegaard* (New York: Garland, 1988), pp. 6-7.

[2]Laura M. Carpenter, *Virginity Lost: An Intimate Portrait of First Sexual Experiences* (New York: New York University Press, 2005).

[3]Seen through the procreative lens, female virginity prior to marriage and sexual exclusivity within marriage is important in ensuring that the paternity of offspring is known; male sexual exclusivity according to Thomas Aquinas's procreative view, a matter of parity and justice. To ask women to have only one sexual partner but not make the same requirement of men would, he thought, be unfair. See Saint Thomas Aquinas, *Summa Conta Gentiles Book Three: Divine Providence Part II,* trans. Vernon J. Bourke (Notre Dame: University of Notre Dame Press, 1975), p. 151.

[4]Carpenter, *Virginity Lost,* pp. 196-97.

[5]Ibid., p. 196.

[6]Ibid., p. 195.

[7]Ibid., p. 197.

[8]Kathleen Norris, *The Cloister Walk* (New York: Riverhead, 1996), pp. 186-209.

[9]Ibid., pp. 192-93.

[10]Naomi Wolf, *Promiscuities: The Secret Struggle for Womanhood* (New York: Random House, 1997), p. 138.

[11]Lauren F. Winner, *Real Sex: The Naked Truth about Chastity* (Grand Rapids: Brazos, 2005), p. 154.

[12]Aristotle's *Nicomachean Ethics* contains the most well-known account of this theory.

[13]For examples of contemporary virtue theory see Alasdair MacIntyre, *After Virtue* (Notre Dame: Notre Dame University Press, 1981); Robert B. Kruschwitz and Robert C. Roberts, *The Virtues: Contemporary Essays on Moral Character* (Belmont, Calif.: Wadsworth, 1987); Rosalind Hursthouse, *On Virtue Ethics* (New York: Oxford University Press, 1999); Robert C. Roberts, *Spiritual Emotions: A Psychology of Christian Virtues* (Grand Rapids: Eerdmans, 2007).

[14]Winner, *Real Sex,* p. 123.

[15]Ibid.

[16]Jozef D. Zalot and Benedict Guevin, OSB, *Catholic Ethics in Today's World* (Winona, Minn.: Saint Mary's Press, 2008), p. 233. This still has a behav-

ioral component, for the authors go on to characterize chastity as "recognizing what sexuality is for and conforming our actions to it."

[17]Grabowski, *Sex and Virtue*, p. 85. Grabowski is actually referencing material written by John Paul II while he was still Cardinal Karol Wojtyla.

[18]Susan Moore and Doreen Rosenthal, *Sexuality in Adolescence* (New York: Routledge, 2006), p. 237.

[19]Grabowski, *Sex and Virtue*, p. 89.

[20]Saint Augustine, *Confessions,* trans. Henry Chadwick (New York: Oxford University Press, 1991), p. 145.

[21]"The virtue of chastity, whose function it is to free love from utilitarian attitudes, must control not only sensuality and carnal concupiscence, as such, but—perhaps more important—those centers deep within the human being in which the utilitarian attitude is hatched and grows. . . . To be chaste means to have a 'transparent' attitude to a person of the other sex—*chastity means just that—the interior 'transparency'* without which love is not itself, for it cannot be itself until the desire to 'enjoy' is subordinate to a readiness to show loving kindness in every situation." Karol Wojtyla (Pope John Paul II), *Love and Responsibility,* trans. H. T. Willetts (San Francisco: Ignatius, 1993), p. 170.

[22]Winner, *Real Sex,* p. 26.

Chapter 4: Flirtation and Seduction

[1]In ordinary usage, the distinction that I am drawing between flirtation and seduction is not consistently encoded in these very words. A flirt who is exploitive of others is often called a tease; *seduction* is often used in a neutral or even positive way to denote sexual wooing whether or not it circumvents the sexual autonomy of another. What is important for sexual insight is not the terminology used but the important ethical and spiritual distinction between respectful explorations and stimulations of sexual interest and exploitive manipulation. I am using "innocent flirtation" for the former and "seduction" for the latter, while acknowledging a stretch of gray area along the continuum between these.

[2]Adam Phillips, *On Flirtation* (Cambridge, Mass.: Harvard University Press, 1994), p. xxiii.

[3]Moore and Rosenthal, *Sexuality in Adolescence,* p. 116.

[4]Ibid.

[5]Roger Scruton, *Sexual Desire: A Moral Philosophy of the Erotic* (New York: Free Press, 1986), p. 145-46.

[6]Katie Roiphe, "Reckless Eyeballing: Sexual Harassment on Campus," in *Sexual Harassment: Issues and Answers,* ed. Linda LeMoncheck and James P.

Sterba (New York: Oxford University Press, 2001), p. 250.

[7]See Joshua Harris's *I Kissed Dating Goodbye,* updated ed. (Portland: Multnomah, 2003), for a conservative covenantal critique of dating and flirtation.

[8]Thomas Nagel, "Sexual Perversion," in *Mortal Questions,* ed. Thomas Nagel (New York: Cambridge University Press, 1979), p. 47.

[9]Ibid., p. 45.

[10]Ibid., p. 49.

[11]Christopher Hampton, *Les Liaisons Dangereuses* (Boston: Faber and Faber, 1987).

[12]Portions of the following section are from Caroline J. Simon, "Seduction: Does How You Get to 'Yes' Still Matter?" in *Philosophy, Feminism and Faith,* ed. Marya Bower and Ruth Groenhout (Bloomington: Indiana University Press, 2003), pp. 180-82.

[13]Hampton, *Les Liaisons Dangereuses,* p. 11.

[14]Ibid., p. 13.

[15]Ibid., pp. 73-74.

[16]Onora O'Neill, "Between Consenting Adults," *Philosophy and Public Affairs* 14 (1985): 270.

Chapter 5: Homosexuality

[1]Two relevant examples of writers on this issue who do not fall into neat conservative or liberal categories are psychologist David G. Myers (coauthor with Letha Dawson Scanzoni of *What God Has Joined Together: A Christian Case for Gay Marriage* [San Francisco: HarperSanFrancisco, 2005]), who espouses a profamily, pro-gay-marriage position, and New Testament scholar Richard B. Hays, who thinks that gays who are Christians should be celibate but should have full civil rights regardless of their sexual activities and should not be barred from Christian ordination (see his *The Moral Vision of the New Testament: A Contemporary Introduction to New Testament Ethics* [San Francisco: HarperSanFrancisco, 1996], pp. 400-403).

[2]See, for example, Benedict J. Groeschel, *The Courage to Be Celibate* (New York: Paulist Press, 1985), pp. 31-32, 48-54.

[3]Raina Kelley, "How Long Will This Take?" *Newsweek,* August 16, 2010, p. 52.

[4]Anna Quindlen, "The Loving Decision," *Newsweek,* November 15, 2008, p. 68.

[5]Ibid.

[6]For various views of how to conceptualize this spectrum, see David P. McWhirter, June Machover Reinisch and Stephanie A. Sanders, eds., *Homosexuality/Heterosexuality: Concepts of Sexual Orientation* (New York: Oxford University Press, 1990).

[7]Myers and Scanzoni state that "Only about one in two hundred sexually active respondents in anonymous national surveys [in the United States and in the Netherlands] . . . report having both male and female partners in the last year." Ibid., p. 53.

[8]www.focusonthefamily.com/socialissues/sexual-identity/progay-revisionist-theology/our-position.aspx.

[9]Hays, *Moral Vision of the New Testament,* p. 390.

[10]Ibid.

[11]Allen D. Verhey, "The Holy Bible and Sanctified Sexuality: An Evangelical Approach to Scripture and Sexual Ethics," *Interpretation* 49, no. 1 (1995): 44. See also Lewis B. Smedes, *Sex for Christians* (Grand Rapids: Eerdmans, 1994), pp. 238-44.

[12]Alice Ogden Bellis, "When God Makes a Way," *The Other Side* (March-April 1995): 44.

[13]Controversies about the implications of a covenantal view for homosexuality, when they are based on debates about an adequate theological anthropology and correct interpretation of the Bible, are internal to Christianity. They have parallels within other religious traditions as well. Jewish theologians, for example, have grappled with these issues and espoused views whose complexities mirror those alluded to above. Those who identify with these religious traditions, and seek to have their lives shaped by them, will want to closely examine the arguments on all sides in order to inform their own convictions. In Saul M. Olyan and Martha C. Nussbaum, eds., *Sexual Orientation and Human Rights in American Religious Discourse* (New York: Oxford University Press, 1998), the authors consider a spectrum of positions taken within the Jewish, Roman Catholic, mainline Protestant and African American Christian communities. The collection shows that there are liberal and conservative voices within each of these traditions.

[14]Suzanne Pharr, "Homophobia and Sexism," in *Experiencing Race, Class and Gender in the United States,* ed. Virginia Cyrus, 2nd ed. (Mountain View, Calif.: Mayfield, 1993), p. 293.

[15]Gwyn Kirk and Margo Okazawa-Rey, "Theory and Theorizing: Integrated Frameworks for Understanding," in *Women's Lives: Multicultural Perspectives,* ed. Gwyn Kirk and Margo Okazawa-Rey (Mountain View, Calif.: Mayfield, 1998), p. 12.

Chapter 6: Casual Sex

[1]Russell Vannoy, *Sex without Love: A Philosophical Exploration* (Buffalo: Prometheus, 1980).

[2]Immanuel Kant, *Foundations of the Metaphysics of Morals,* trans. Lewis

White Beck (Upper Saddle River, N.J.: Prentice Hall, 1997). For examples of contemporary Kantian and duty-based ethics see Onora O'Neill, *An Essay on Kantian Ethics* (New York: Columbia University Press, 1975); Alan Donagan, *The Theory of Morality* (Chicago: University of Chicago Press, 1977); Christine M. Korsgaard, *Creating the Kingdom of Ends* (Cambridge: Cambridge University Press, 1996).

[3]Jeremy Bentham, *Introduction to the Principles of Morals and Legislation* (Oxford: Oxford University Press, 1948); John Stuart Mill, *Utilitarianism* (Upper Saddle River, N.J.: Prentice Hall, 1957). For contemporary consequentialist accounts see Anthony Quinton's *Utilitarian Ethics* (London: Duckworth, 1989), and R. M. Hare, *Moral Thinking* (New York: Oxford University Press, 1981).

[4]One can, however, be a consequentialist without holding that pain and pleasure are the only or the most important consequences to take into account in ethical thinking. Some would hold that knowledge or beauty, for example, are valuable in themselves, apart from causing pleasure and despite causing pain.

[5]Donna Freitas, *Sex and the Soul* (New York: Oxford University Press, 2008), p. 150.

[6]Marquis de Sade, *Marquis de Sade: The Complete Justine, Philosophy of the Bedroom, and Other Writings,* comp. and trans. Richard Seaver and Austryn Wainshouse (New York: Grove, 1965), p. 319.

[7]David Archard, *Sexual Consent* (Boulder, Colo.: Westview, 1998). The book's working hypothesis is that consent is the only morally relevant consideration governing our sexual behavior. This is not an assumption that the procreative or covenantal or romantic views will agree with, but Archard's project will be relevant to those of us who hold these views nonetheless. It can help us understand the importance of consent, even if consent is only a necessary but not a sufficient condition for appropriate sexual behavior. In what follows, I will be expositing those parts of Archard's account that I find most illuminating (he makes other assertions that I find problematic but will not be sorting those out in this book).

[8]Among the stipulations of the policy are "Each new level of sexual activity requires consent," "Use of agreed upon forms of communication such as gestures or safe words is acceptable, but must be discussed and verbally agreed to by all parties before sexual activity occurs," and "Body movements and non-verbal responses such as moans are not consent," http://antiochmedia.org/mirror/antiwarp/www.antioch-college.edu/Campus/sopp/index.html.

[9]Archard, *Sexual Consent,* p. 144.

[10] Ogden Nash, "Reflections on Ice-Breaking," *The Face Is Familiar* (Garden City, N.Y.: Garden City Publishers, 1941), p. 259.

[11] Seiriol Morgan, "Sex in the Head," *Journal of Applied Philosophy* 20 (2003): 1-16.

[12] Wolf, *Promiscuities,* p. 177.

[13] Ibid., p. 223.

[14] Robert C. Solomon, "Sexual Paradigms," *Journal of Philosophy* 71, no. 11 (1974): 344.

[15] Janis Moulton, "Sexual Behavior: Another Position," *Journal of Philosophy* 73, no. 16 (1976): 545.

[16] Moore and Rosenthal, *Sexuality in Adolescence,* p. 144.

[17] Ibid.

[18] Primoratz, *Ethics and Sex,* pp. 32-33.

[19] Alan Goldman, for example, asserts, "I am not suggesting here that sex ought never to be connected with love or that it is not a more significant and valuable activity when it is." In "Plain Sex," *Philosophy and Public Affairs* 6 (1977): 274.

[20] John Hunter, "Sex and Personal Intimacy," in *Moral Issues,* ed. Jan Narveson (New York: Oxford University Press, 1983), p. 298.

[21] See Hera Cook, *The Long Sexual Revolution: English Women, Sex, and Contraception 1800–1975* (New York: Oxford University Press, 2004).

[22] Kristjan Kristjansson, "Casual Sex Revisted," *Journal of Social Philosophy* 29, no. 2 (1998): 99, 104.

[23] Ibid., p. 104.

[24] Immanuel Kant, *Lectures on Ethics,* trans. Louis Infield (London: Methuen, 1930), p. 164.

[25] Ibid., p. 165.

[26] Ibid., p. 167.

Chapter 7: Sex as a Commodity

[1] Susan J. Douglas, *The Rise of Enlightened Sexism: How Pop Culture Took Us from Girl Power to Girls Gone Wild* (New York: St. Martin's Griffin, 2010).

[2] The commodification of sex has ramifications well beyond prostitution and pornography. Sex has become the ultimate adjunct to market capitalism; sexualized images are used to sell everything from cars to sports teams. (I owe this observation to the Rev. Dr. David Sinclair.)

[3] Martha C. Nussbaum, "'Whether from Reason or Prejudice': Taking Money for Bodily Services," in *Sex and Social Justice* (New York: Oxford University Press, 1999), p. 277.

[4] See chapter three, p. 75.

[5]See, for example, Sallie Tisdale's memoir *Talk Dirty to Me.* (New York: Anchor Books, 1995).

[6]Catherine MacKinnon, *Feminism Unmodified* (Cambridge, Mass.: Harvard University Press, 1987), pp. 148-62.

[7]Naomi Wolf, "The Porn Myth," http://nymag.com/nymetro/news/trends/n_9437/.

[8]Carole Pateman, "Defending Prostitution: Charges Against Ericsson," *Ethics* 93, no. 3 (1983): 564. Pateman is responding to arguments in Lars O. Ericsson, "Charges Against Prostitution: An Attempt at a Philosophical Assessment," *Ethics* 90, no. 3 (1980): 335-66. Ericsson presents what I've called the perennial plain sex defense of prostitution.

[9]Wolf, *Promiscuities,* p. 81.

[10]Yolanda Estes, "Prostitution: A Subjective Position," in *The Philosophy of Sex: Contemporary Readings,* ed. Alan Soble and Nicholas Power (Lanham, Md.: Rowman & Littlefield, 2008), p. 357.

[11]S. E. Marshall, "Bodyshopping: The Case of Prostitution," *Journal of Applied Philosophy* 16, no. 2 (1999): 145. The article by Martha Nussbaum to which Marshall is indebted is "Objectification," *Philosophy and Public Affairs* 24, no. 4 (1995): 257.

[12]Marshall, "Bodyshopping," p. 145.

[13]Ibid., p. 146.

[14]Catharine A. MacKinnon, "A Feminist/Political Approach: Pleasure Under Patriarchy," in *Theories of Human Sexuality,* ed. James H. Geer and William T. O'Donohue (New York: Plenum, 1987), p. 78.

[15]Ibid., p. 69.

[16]MacKinnon, *Feminism Unmodified,* p. 172. See also Judith M. Hill, "Pornography and Degradation," *Hypatia* 2, no. 2 (1987): 39-54.

[17]Harry Brod, "Pornography and the Alienation of Male Sexuality," in *Moral Controversies: Race, Class and Gender in Applied Ethics,* ed. Steven Jay Gold (Belmont, Calif.: Wadsworth, 1993), p. 374.

[18]Ibid.

[19]Joan Mason-Grant, "Pornography as Embodied Practice," in *The Philosophy of Sex: Contemporary Readings,* ed. Alan Soble and Nicholas Power (Lanham, Md.: Rowman & Littlefield, 2008), p. 414.

[20]Ibid., p. 412.

[21]Brod, "Pornography and Alienation," p. 379.

[22]I am not advocating either the decriminalization of prostitution or the criminalization of casual sex—any such recommendation would need a careful consideration of the relationship between morality and legality, as well as the purpose of law in a well-ordered society. What I am advocating

is a deeper level of moral reflection and a more vigorous conversation on matters of sexual behavior than are widespread in our culture or among Christians at the present time.

Conclusion: Toward Sexual Integrity

[1]Berry, "Sex, Economy, Freedom, and Community," p. 122.

[2]Annie Dillard, "An Expedition to the Pole," in *Teaching a Stone to Talk* (New York: Harper & Row, 1982), p. 30.

[3]C. S. Lewis, *Surprised by Joy* (New York: Harcourt, Brace, 1955), pp. 17-18.